Understanding LIVING TRUSTS®

How to Avoid Probate, Save Taxes and More.

A complete information &
planning guide written in easy to
understand, conversational English.

New Expanded Second Edition

By Vickie Schumacher and Jim Schumacher

Published by Schumacher And Company, Los Angeles CA

PLEASE READ THIS: We have done our best to give you useful and accurate information concerning the subject matter covered in this publication. However, please be aware that laws and procedures are constantly changing and are subject to differing interpretations. This book is intended to give an overview of the information presented and should never be used as a substitute for seeking expert advice. It is sold with the understanding that the publisher and the authors are not engaged in rendering legal, accounting or other professional service. If legal advice or other expert assistance is required, the services of a competent professional should be sought.

Published by Schumacher And Company.

First printing: May, 1990
Second printing: August, 1990
Third printing: January, 1991
Fourth printing: April, 1991
Fifth printing: July, 1991
Sixth printing: September, 1991
Seventh printing: March, 1992
Eighth printing: August, 1992
Ninth printing: January, 1993
Tenth printing: May, 1993

First edition published March, 1988 as *A Will Is Not The Way—The Living Trust Alternative* and *Avoid Probate—The Living Trust Alternative*.

This publication is available for bulk purchases. For information:
Schumacher And Company
1800 Century Park East, Suite 1250
Los Angeles, California 90067
(310) 284-8866

ISBN 0-945811-07-1

Library of Congress Catalog Card Number: 89-92798
Printed in the United States of America.

This book is lovingly dedicated to our first child
James Price Schumacher II
whose early arrival immediately put our lives into perspective—
and totally disrupted our schedule for releasing this book!

Thank you, JJ, for being so happy, good-natured and patient
with us. We hope you continue to be delighted with
each new experience and person you meet.
(He hopes this book sells lots of copies so he can go to college!)

ABOUT THE AUTHORS

Vickie and Jim Schumacher are the principals of Schumacher And Company in Los Angeles, a corporate communications firm that specializes in "translating" legal and financial information into clear, conversational English. Their primary areas of expertise are employee benefits/ executive compensation and trust communications.

Vickie Schumacher is an award-winning writer, nationally recognized for her abilities to communicate "legalese" in accurate and understandable English, and to create an inviting and easy-to-read format. She is a former regional head of communications for a major employee benefits firm, and has been a senior consultant for others.

Jim Schumacher is a former sales and marketing executive with a Fortune 100 company. He is responsible for shifting the company's focus to producing and marketing living trust communications to both the public and professionals. In addition to creating new products with Vickie, Jim oversees all sales and marketing activities for the company.

Vickie and Jim are co-authors of the book *A Will Is Not The Way—The Living Trust Alternative* (also titled *Avoid Probate—The Living Trust Alternative*), which sold more than 50,000 copies since its release in 1988.

CONTRIBUTING EDITORS

The authors would like to thank the following individuals who acted as technical advisors and reviewers for this book.

Edward A. Setzler is a Partner in the Kansas City, Missouri law firm of Spencer, Fane, Britt and Browne. He is past President of the Estate Planning Society of Kansas City, past Chairman of the Probate and Trust Committee of the Kansas City Bar Association and is a Fellow of The American College of Trust and Estate Counsel. Mr. Setzler is a frequent lecturer on estate planning and probate matters for the Continuing Legal Education Department of the University of Missouri at Kansas City Law School and for the Missouri Bar Association. He is co-editor or co-author for the Missouri Bar Association Deskbooks on Estate Planning, Probate, Trusts and Guardianships, and is listed in the books *Best Lawyers in America* and *Who's Who in American Law.*

Marshal A. Oldman is a Partner in the Encino, California law firm of Cappadona and Oldman, specializing in probate and estate planning. He is currently President of the San Fernando Valley Bar Association and is a Past Chairman of the Probate Sections of the Los Angeles County Bar Association and the San Fernando Valley Bar Association. He has been active in monitoring probate legislation on behalf of the Los Angeles County Bar and is a frequent lecturer to lawyer and community groups regarding changes in probate and estate tax legislation.

SPECIAL THANKS

Shela Camenisch
Doug Freeman
Kenneth Leventhal
Jim Normandin
Ken Adler
Matthew Mack

Extra Special Thanks

Jasmine Murata	For art direction, design, illustration and patience (just *one* more change) in making this book look so good (Go Bruins!)
Lynne Mackechnie	For trying to keep us all "together"
Marr Leisure	Without whose encouragement, support and general harassment we probably wouldn't be doing this at all!

And, of course, to the many people who read the first edition of our book—especially those who took the time to write or call us. Your praise, suggestions and questions spurred us on to write this expanded, second edition. Thank you!

INTRODUCTION

Have you made plans to distribute your property and take care of your family when you die or if you become incompetent? If so, you probably used a will or joint ownership. Or maybe you haven't done anything (that's not unusual). Any of these traditional estate planning methods (and doing nothing is *very* traditional) can work. But they all have risks, and sooner or later will lead to probate.

Unfortunately, most people don't realize what this can mean until it's too late. We wrote this book because we want you to know about these risks now, and what can happen to you, your family and your property in probate. For example, did you know:

- A will does not avoid probate?
- Probate costs can consume up to 10% *or more* of the gross value of your estate?
- The probate process usually takes at least a year, and often longer?
- Probate files are public record and anyone can have access to your file?
- Your will can easily be contested?
- You and your property can be placed under the control of the probate court *before* you die?
- You may not be able to sell jointly owned property without approval from the probate court?
- The probate court—not your child's guardian—will probably control your child's inheritance?

Did you also know there is another traditional estate planning alternative that avoids all probate and lets you keep complete control, even if you become physically or mentally incapacitated? It's called a *living trust*. With a properly prepared living trust, you can have the security of knowing that your plan will *stay* your plan—it won't be altered by the court, greedy relatives or unforeseen legal technicalities.

Before we tell you more, there are a few things about this book we'd like you to know. First, we wrote this book for you, the public. We have written it in clear, conversational English and have intentionally avoided the use of technical legal terms wherever possible.

Second, we are presenting this information as a general overview. We haven't gotten bogged down with specific laws and regulations, complicated tax discussions or every conceivable situation that could come up. You may find some minor variations in your state's laws, but generally these will only be technical and won't affect the overall message.

Third, this book is not a "do-it-yourselfer." These generic estate planning books can't address the unique needs of different families in different states. In fact, using them can be very dangerous. While we definitely feel the legal profession could be doing more to inform the public and meet its needs (which would eliminate much of this do-it-yourself market), we feel very strongly that you need guidance from an experienced and conscientious estate planning attorney.

In closing, we don't think it's right that so many families continue to go through probate just because they're not informed—they don't know what can happen in probate or that they can avoid it entirely with a living trust. We believe you need to know, and you need accurate and understandable information. That's why we wrote this book. At least now you will have enough good information so *you* can choose what's best for your family—before it's too late.

TABLE OF CONTENTS

GOOD PLANS CAN GO WRONG

GOOD PLANS CAN GO WRONG

Mary was a widow with no children or immediate family. In her will, she left everything in equal shares to three institutions which had been a big part of her life—to her husband's university for scholarships in his memory, to her neighborhood church and to a children's hospital, where her only child had been treated for a terminal illness many years earlier.

When Mary died, her will had to be probated before her property could be given to the institutions. As required by law, a notice of her death was published in the newspaper and a list of her assets was made public. Some distant relatives (who Mary barely knew) saw the notice in the paper, hired an attorney and filed a lawsuit. They claimed Mary was incompetent when she signed her will, so it was invalid. The institutions had to hire attorneys to try and uphold Mary's will, and Mary's estate also had to be represented by an attorney. A nasty and expensive legal battle began. Finally, more than four years later, the institutions agreed to give Mary's relatives half of her estate, just to end the fight. This was obviously not what Mary had wanted.

Betty, recently divorced, had a 3 year old daughter named Sarah. She had heard she should have a will (especially since she had a child), and when she saw an advertisement for a will kit, she ordered one through the mail. In her will, she left everything to Sarah. She didn't have that much property, so she increased her life insurance and listed Sarah as beneficiary. She named her sister Linda as Sarah's guardian, thinking Linda would be able to use the life insurance money to raise Sarah if something happened to her.

A few years later, Betty was killed in a car accident and her will went through probate. Because Sarah was a minor, the court had to establish a probate guardianship for her. The court did allow Linda to be Sarah's guardian, but the court kept control of the inheritance—everything Betty left Sarah in her will *and* the money from the life insurance company (which would not pay directly to Sarah because she was under age). When Sarah turned 18, the legal age in that state, she received all of her inheritance in one lump sum, which she quickly spent in one year of expensive living.

Betty's will kit did not inform her that the court, not the guardian, would have control of the inheritance, that most insurance companies will not pay benefits directly to a minor child, *or* that a minor receives the full inheritance when he/ she reaches legal age.

Dorothy, a widow, put all of her property, including her house, into joint ownership with her married son. She did this thinking that, when she died, her property would automatically go to her son without the need for probate. Several years later, her son and his wife separated and Dorothy decided to sell her house so she could move in with her son. But she soon discovered she could not sell it without her *daughter-in-law's* signature on the deed. The daughter-in-law was still legally married to her son and was entitled by law to a "marital interest" in the property. The title company would not insure clear title to the buyer without the daughter-in-law's signature because it wasn't clear what her "interest" would be—and she refused to sign unless she got part of the money when the house was sold. Dorothy was stuck—she didn't know that joint ownership with a married person can include *that person's spouse*. And because Dorothy had placed her house in joint ownership, she lost control of her own home.

On the advice of a neighbor, Frank and Elizabeth, an elderly couple, put everything they owned, including their home and stocks, in their adult unmarried daughter's name. They believed that this would avoid probate and that all their property would pass directly to their daughter—their only child—when they were both gone. A year later, Frank died of a heart attack. Several months after that, their daughter was suddenly killed in an auto accident.

Elizabeth never thought that she would survive both her husband and daughter. To add to her distress, Elizabeth now owned nothing in her own name—everything was in her daughter's name. She was forced to probate her daughter's estate to get back her own property. During this long process she had to rely on the court to grant her living expenses. Sometimes the court would approve them, sometimes not. And during a declining stock market, she helplessly watched the value of her stocks fall to only a fraction of their previous value because the court could not react in time for them to be sold quickly enough. Elizabeth lost her financial independence plus a substantial portion of her assets to probate—just trying to get back what was hers in the first place.

John and Ellen had each been married before and had young children from their first marriages. When they married, they considered it a fresh start and one family. They put all of their property in both their names (joint ownership), with the intention that when they died, all the children would receive an equal share. They didn't do a will because they thought joint ownership would serve the same purpose.

When John died, everything went to Ellen and she continued to raise and care for all the children. When Ellen died many years later, her property had to go through probate. Under the probate laws of that state, Ellen's property could only be distributed to *her surviving blood children*. Since John's children had never been legally adopted by Ellen, they received nothing. Even though John and Ellen thought of all the children as being their own, the probate laws did not. Because they relied on joint ownership, they unknowingly disinherited John's children.

When Edward and Beth married, they both had children and property from previous marriages. They had new wills drawn up, with each leaving the property they had acquired before their marriage to their own children. Edward's will left title of his 300-acre family farm to his children.

Edward died ten years later. While his will was in probate, Beth's attorney advised her that, as a surviving spouse in the state in which she lived, she was entitled to a percentage of all of Edward's property, including the farm. Although Beth knew that Edward had wanted the farm to go solely to his children, she felt that she and her children had a right to part of it and decided to contest Edward's will. This prompted a bitter court battle, with Beth and her children on one side, and Edward's children on the other. Eventually, Beth won and was granted a percentage of the farm, but the closeness the family had established during Edward's lifetime was destroyed. Edward's will offered no protection to his children and did not guarantee that his wishes would be carried out.

Claire was very lonely after Fred, her husband of forty years, died. To fill her time, she started taking ballroom dancing lessons. Her instructor, a much younger South American "gentleman," was very quick to provide her with the companionship she was missing and Claire, with a new sense of self-esteem, soon fell head over heels. Fred and Claire's children were shocked when their mother announced she had married her instructor. But the real shock came seven months later when Claire died—and the children learned their mother had placed everything in joint ownership with her new husband. As the new sole owner, he decided to sell everything and left town. Because their mother had made her new husband joint owner, the children had been completely disinherited. And everything Fred and Claire had built over the years had gone south—south of the border.

Doris and Bob owned a family-style restaurant. They had been moderately successful for years, and put everything they made back into the business. When Bob died, one of their competitors went down to the probate court and looked up his file. In it he found much of Bob and Doris' financial information—a list of all their assets, restaurant equipment, debts, bank accounts—a competitor's dream. He also saw in the file that Doris was short on cash, and had requested a living allowance from the court. And it looked like she was going to have to sell some of their assets to pay the attorney's fees. He offered to buy Doris out—at 50% of what he knew the restaurant was worth. To his amazement, she accepted, without any negotiation. This competitor had "inside information"—courtesy of the probate files.

John and Eleanor had planned carefully, saved and invested wisely for their retirement. They made sure their wills, which left everything to each other, were always up to date; they even had trusts in their wills for extra protection.

A living trust would have prevented all these situations

Unfortunately, John developed Alzheimer's disease. As his condition worsened, Eleanor had to sell some of their investments to support them and pay for his care. But because they owned everything jointly, Eleanor soon found out she needed John's signature to sell. However, John was no longer able to conduct business, and Eleanor was forced to have him declared incompetent and placed in a court-supervised conservatorship. Now, in addition to dealing with John's condition, Eleanor had to deal with the court which insisted upon approving all expenses and the sale of any of their investments. Eleanor had never had to handle their finances before and she often felt confused, frustrated, frightened—and alone.

When John died, Eleanor found herself back in probate court again—this time to probate John's will. Through the public notices, one of John's brothers found out about the proceedings and appeared "from nowhere" to contest the will. After several years of expensive bickering back and forth, Eleanor finally decided to give him part of John's estate—before it was all gone.

Eleanor and John did plan carefully—but they didn't avoid probate. They didn't know their wills provided no protection if one of them became incapacitated, that their wills had to be probated before their trusts could even go into effect, or that their wills would be made public and could be contested so easily.

A living trust would have easily prevented all of these unexpected situations, and many others like them!

Part One

ALL ABOUT PROBATE

Part One —

ALL ABOUT PROBATE

Before you can appreciate the advantages of a living trust, you have to understand what can happen to you and your family in probate. Just about everyone has heard of probate, but most people really don't know what it can mean—until it's too late to do anything about it. In this section, we'll tell you all about probate so you can learn about it without having to experience it first-hand—and still have the time to avoid it with a living trust.

THE TRUTH ABOUT PROBATE

What Is Probate?

Probate is the legal process through which your bills are paid and your property is distributed when you die based upon what your will says (if you have one) or what the law says (if you don't). Probate also takes control for those who cannot handle their own affairs because they are incompetent or are minor children. The court will step in and control their financial and personal affairs while they are not able to take care of themselves—until the incompetent person recovers or dies, or until the minor child legally becomes an adult.

Probate is the only way to legally transfer title to any titled property (such as real estate, car, bank accounts, etc.) when the person listed as the owner cannot sign his/her name due to death or incompetency, or because he/she is a minor.

Why Does Probate Exist?

Probate has existed in one form or another for hundreds of years. It was created with the best intentions to protect you, your property and your family.

Probate

Without a living trust, all of your property (including your personal possessions) must go through probate, and all expenses must be paid, before anything can go to your heirs.

It provided an orderly method of paying bills and transferring ownership of property at death, and for managing the financial affairs of an incompetent person or minor child—all under direct supervision of the court system.

The probate process is obsolete

So, What's Wrong With Probate?

The probate process is simply obsolete. Probate was, and still is, a very *slow* and cumbersome process. It is a product of the "horse and carriage days," when it took months to locate and notify relatives (and creditors) of a death or illness in the family. Back then it didn't matter that probate took a long time—but today it does. Things move much more quickly today. We can communicate with friends and relatives anywhere in the world in just seconds, and many times financial decisions must be made within hours. Times have changed, but probate has not. In California, for example, the average probate takes two years, and some cases go on for five years and longer.

Besides taking a long time, probate is expensive and inflexible. Once the process begins, you and your family lose control, and the court takes over. Probate is a complicated legal process. It can only go by exactly what the law tells it to do, and only when the law says to do it. Probate—with its inflexibility, costs and painstakingly slow process—can cause all kinds of unexpected and unnecessary problems for today's families.

When Probate Can Get You

Very simply, unless you take the proper action now, probate can and probably will affect you and your family in at least one of the following three ways:

1. When you die
2. If you become incompetent
3. If your minor children inherit property

There are only two sure ways to avoid probate. Own nothing in your own name, not even a bank account—and how many of us would that include? Or you can get a living trust.

In Part One, we'll look at how you and your family can end up under the control of the probate court in each of these three situations, and what happens if you do. But first, let's look at some traditional methods people use to try and avoid probate—and why, in many cases, they don't work the way people think they will.

COMMON MYTHS ABOUT AVOIDING PROBATE

Myth 1: "I have a will, so my family won't have to go through probate when I die."

False—Having a will does *not* avoid probate. In fact, a will is a one-way ticket to probate.

A will can have no effect unless it goes through the probate process—it *must* be admitted to the probate court to be legal and enforceable. Your will must be validated as being authentic before ownership of your assets can be transferred to your heirs, and the probate court is the only way this can be done—that's its job. So, if you have a will, you are telling your family that you want them to go through probate.

Problems With Handwritten And Other Do-It-Yourself Wills

In addition to having to go through probate, you could run into other problems if you write your own will, either in your own handwriting (called *a holographic* will) or if you use a "do-it-yourself" mail order will kit (you've probably seen these advertised on late-night television and in magazines). State laws vary widely (some do not even accept a handwritten will), and unless you know *exactly* what you are doing, the slightest technical error can cause your will to be thrown out by the court. If your will is accepted as valid, one slight error could create some ridiculous problems. Here's an example:

> Recently an elderly woman died in Los Angeles and in her "do-it-yourself" will, which was accepted by the court as valid, she left a substantial sum to the "University of Southern California" which goes by the initials "USC." But later on in her will she referred to this institution as "UCLA," which just happens to be the cross-town rival. College sports fans will especially appreciate this controversy—attorneys from both institutions will be battling this one out for some time.

Myth 2: "My will has a trust in it, so it won't have to go through probate."

False—Many people think that if they have a trust in their will, the trust lets them avoid probate. But, as we just explained, *all* wills—even those with trusts in them—must go through probate. The trust can't go into effect until *after* the will has been probated.

Myth 3: "I don't have a will, so there will be no need for my family to go through probate when I die."

False, again—Even if *you* haven't written a will, *the state has written one for you.* Every state has laws for the distribution of property for those who die without a will. So, if you don't have a will when you die (or if your will is not accepted by the court), the state has to make sure your debts are paid and your property is distributed *according to the laws of that state*—which may or may not be the way you would have wanted. Consider, for example, the true story of the famous movie actor James Dean:

A will is a one-way ticket to probate

> His mother died when he was a small child, and his father sent him to live with an aunt and uncle who raised him. James, who had grown very close to his "new" family, had talked about wanting his aunt and uncle to receive most of his property if something happened to him, and particularly had expressed wanting to provide for his young cousin's college education—but he never got around to making out a will. When he was killed suddenly in a car accident, his estate went through probate. Since he did not have a will, his property was distributed according to California law (the *state's will*). Everything he owned was given to his father because he was his closest surviving relative, even though there had been little contact between them over the years. Under the terms of the state's will, his aunt and uncle (who had devoted years of their lives to raising and loving him) and his cousin received nothing.

Myth 4: "I own everything jointly, so when I die all my property will immediately go to the other owner without probate."

Maybe, but look out! Joint ownership does not guarantee that you will avoid probate. In fact, usually it just *postpones* it—and it can create all kinds of unexpected, and unwanted, problems.

The kind of joint ownership most people have is called "joint tenancy with right of survivorship." This means that when one of the owners dies, his/her share instantly becomes the property of the surviving joint owner. It is often used by spouses (husbands and wives) or between parents and their adult children, thinking they will avoid probate—and in many situations it does work. For example, if both your and your spouse's names are on the titles of all the property you own, ownership will immediately transfer to the surviving spouse when one of you dies, without probate.

Joint ownership causes all kinds of unexpected problems

Unanticipated Problems

But joint ownership can throw you some unexpected curves. Let's say, for example, you successfully use joint ownership to avoid probate and transfer your share to your surviving spouse when you die, but for some reason your spouse doesn't add another joint owner (which frequently happens). When your spouse dies, the entire estate (your spouse's estate plus what you left your spouse) must go through probate before ownership can be transferred to the rest of your heirs. So you didn't *avoid* probate after all—you just *postponed* it.

Also, if you and your spouse die at the same time (say, in a car accident), your jointly owned property would *have* to be probated before it could go to your heirs, whether or not you have a will. And while this isn't *likely* to happen, it very well *could* happen.

Unintentional Disinheriting

Joint ownership can also cause you to unintentionally disinherit your own family. Remember, if you own property jointly with your spouse and you die first, ownership of that property will go to your spouse when you die. And when your spouse dies, the entire property (including your share) will go to your spouse's heirs. That's because when you died, your ownership share automatically transferred to your spouse—so now your spouse owns it outright. You and your heirs no longer have any ownership interest in the property.

Now this may not be a problem if this is the only marriage for both of you which produced children—in this case, your spouse's heirs are also yours. But what if you have children from a previous marriage? Unless your spouse had legally adopted them, your children may get nothing—because they are not your spouse's heirs.

Unfortunately, even if you have a will that says you want your children to inherit your share of the jointly owned property, your joint owner (in this case, your spouse) would still receive full ownership. That's because joint ownership acts *immediately* upon the death of one of the owners, so your spouse would own the property outright before your will can even take effect. That means there wouldn't be anything for you "to will" to your children.

Your spouse could include your children in his/her will now, but you still can't be sure they will inherit. Your spouse could always write a new will, disinheriting your children. Or he/she could add another joint owner (like a new spouse) who would then receive full ownership when your spouse dies.

Disinheriting through joint ownership can also be a problem even if you don't have children, because upon your death, your spouse's family (not yours) would inherit the property—even though the property had once been half yours.

Of course, we could go on and on with possible scenarios. The point is that when you make someone else a joint owner with you, you lose control—so you have no guarantees about who will eventually receive your share of the property.

Joint Ownership Can Cause Unintentional Disinheriting

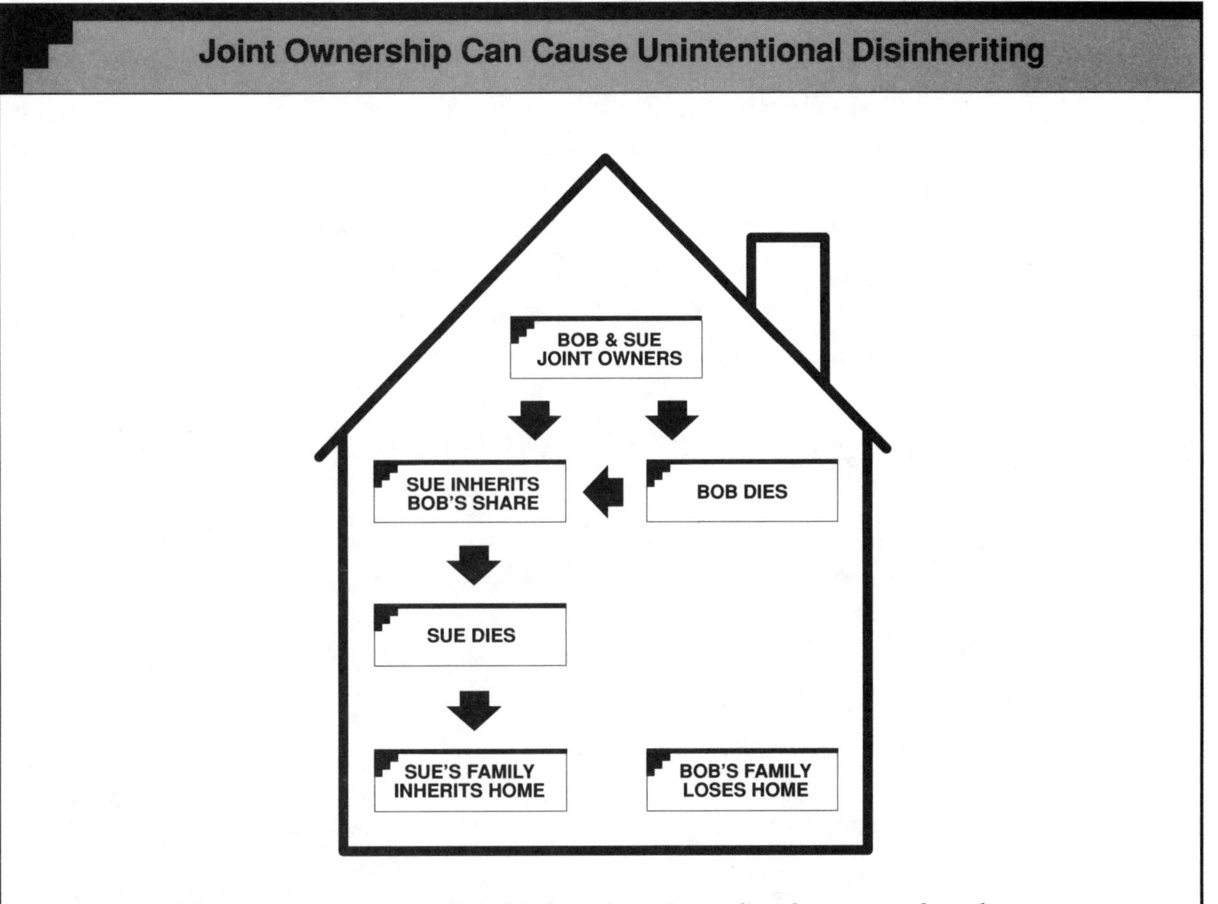

When one joint owner dies, his/her share immediately goes to the other owner. This can cause you to unintentionally disinherit your own family.

Here's one example of how using joint ownership can unintentionally create a disastrous situation:

> Marie, an elderly widow, had a will which left everything in equal shares to her five grown children. When she learned she had cancer, she put everything she owned into joint ownership with her oldest son, thinking this would avoid probate and make things easier for her family when she died. She discussed it with her son and was sure that he would carry out her wishes and divide everything equally among the five children.
>
> When she died, ownership did immediately go to her son. But he died suddenly in a construction accident a few weeks later, *before* the property could be distributed. His wife, only recently married to Marie's son, claimed everything as his surviving spouse, and she decided to keep it all herself! Marie's will (which, remember, left everything in equal shares to her children) could do nothing, because as soon as she died *she no longer owned anything*. Marie's joint ownership plan did avoid probate, but it also disinherited her children!

Physical Or Mental Incapacity

You can really end up in a mess if your joint owner becomes physically or mentally incapacitated and can no longer sign his/her name—especially if real estate is involved. You will have to get approval from the probate court before any jointly owned property can be sold or refinanced—even if your co-owner is your spouse. This whole issue of incapacity (and the involvement of the probate court) is so important and something so few people know about, we've included an entire section on it beginning on page 34.

Potential Lawsuits

You could also end up in a lawsuit. If you are a joint owner with someone who is sued over an incident which involves the jointly owned piece of property, you will very likely be named in the lawsuit, even if you had done nothing. Think about this example:

> Robert and Toni wanted to help their 18 year old son buy a car, so they co-signed the loan and listed themselves as co-owners with their son on the title. Shortly thereafter, the son was at fault in an accident in which the other driver was seriously injured. When the injured person filed suit for

personal injury damages, Robert and Toni were named along with their son. Their personal assets are now at risk—they could be frozen, even seized, to help settle the claim.

Don't become a co-owner and co-signer of a loan. You can guarantee the loan without risking your personal assets. Just think for a moment about how "sue-happy" our society is these days—joint ownership can leave you wide open for a possible lawsuit.

What Kind Of Joint Ownership Do You Have?

Remember, the kind of joint ownership most people have (and the kind we have been discussing) is called "joint tenancy with right of survivorship"—and when one of the joint owners dies, all ownership immediately transfers to the surviving joint owner.

But there is another kind of joint ownership (although not nearly as common) called "tenancy-in-common." Even though it works very differently from "joint tenancy with right of survivorship," people often confuse them. Under tenancy-in-common, when one of the owners dies, that owner's share will legally go to his/her heirs—*not to the other owner*.

If you own property with someone through a tenancy-in-common arrangement, you could find yourself with *several* new co-owners when that person dies and the heirs inherit the property. Sometimes it's hard enough to get two people to agree. Imagine how difficult it could be to get *several* owners to reach an agreement, especially if you are trying to sell a piece of real estate. You could also have the same problems we mentioned earlier (incapacity, lawsuits, etc.). But with *several* owners involved, your risks and problems are multiplied.

Joint Ownership—Is It Worth The Risks?

Maybe joint ownership will work for you—but then again, maybe it won't. With joint ownership, you're playing a kind of "joint ownership roulette" with your family. You could still end up in probate, you could be sued—you could even unintentionally disinherit your own children. Is it worth the risks?

Myth 5: "I'll just give it all away to my children before I die so there won't be anything to probate."

True, there won't be any probate—but, depending on the size of the gift, there may be a gift tax involved. For example, if you transfer $25,000 in stocks to your son or daughter, you are making a gift. And if you make a gift of more than $10,000 per year per person, you have a potential gift tax liability.

Also, if you're giving your children any titled property, you could be giving them a substantial income tax problem. That's because the property you give away would not receive a "stepped-up basis." The "basis" of property is the value which is used to determine gain or loss for income tax purposes—in other words, what you *paid* for it versus what you *receive* for it when it's sold. If you give the property to your children while you are alive, it keeps *your* basis (what you paid for it). But if they receive it as an inheritance (through a will or a trust), it receives a new "stepped-up" basis—and the property is re-valued as of the date of your death.

Here's what this can mean to your children. Let's say you purchased a piece of property in 1945 for $10,000 and it's worth $150,000 when you die. If your children receive it as an inheritance, the basis for this property would now be $150,000. And if they sell it for $150,000, they would pay no income tax. But if you transferred title to your children while you were alive, the basis would be $10,000 (what you paid for it). If they then sold the property for $150,000, they would pay income taxes on the $140,000 gain—about $36,000.

Gifts Do Not Receive A Stepped-Up Basis

	Transfer By Gift While You're Living (No Stepped-Up Basis)	Transfer By Inheritance Through Your Will Or Trust (Stepped-Up Basis)
Selling Price	$150,000	$150,000
Basis	-10,000	-150,000
Gain	$140,000	$0
Estimated Income Tax Due	$36,000	$0

Giving property away can cause tax problems

Now, forget about your children for a moment—and think about yourself. If you completely give away your property, it's gone. What if you decide you want (or need) it back? Things change in families, you know. Your children could sell it against your wishes. Or what if you outlive your children? A daughter (or son) in-law could now have full ownership. Would he/she give it back to you? You could even wind up in probate court, fighting to get your own property back. Substantial gifts (like your home and other real estate) may also disqualify you from receiving Medicaid and Supplemental Security Income (SSI) benefits. You may think this is all very unlikely—but situations just like this happen all too often.

You could "sort of" give it away—by placing it in joint ownership with your children. But you've just read about the risks of joint ownership. Plus you'll probably have to pay a gift tax. And your children may still have an income tax problem to deal with—because only *your* share will get a stepped-up basis to fair market value at your death.

Sound complicated? It certainly can be. Our point is that giving property away just isn't nearly as simple as you may think it is—and it can cause both you and your children some serious tax problems.

Myth 6: "I have a power of attorney, so I don't need a will or joint ownership to avoid probate."

False—Some people give *power of attorney* to a spouse or adult child, thinking it will allow titles of their property to be transferred without probate when they die or if they become physically or mentally incapacitated. But a power of attorney is automatically revoked at death or incapacity, so it won't be of any use then. Some states have a *durable* power of attorney which remains valid through incapacity but it, too, becomes invalid at death. So, in either case, a power of attorney can't be used to change titles after you die.

Sometimes a power of attorney doesn't work at all. Some banks and stock brokerage firms, for example, will not even recognize a power of attorney unless it is on their own form and they *know* this is what their client wants to do. This can be good protection—but it can also be a big problem if you are depending on a power of attorney to work for you.

When a power of attorney does work, it may work so well that it becomes dangerous. Armed with a durable power of attorney, it could be very easy for someone to "raid your estate" if you are incapacitated. This person may be able to transfer titles of your property and accounts to his or her name, and in your condition you probably wouldn't even know about it. You could recover from your incapacity, only to find you have no property or accounts because all of the titles have been changed! You may have a hard time getting your property back—you'll probably have to file a lawsuit, and by the time it's settled there may not be anything left.

With a general power of attorney (which is what most people use), you are simply giving someone else the right to sign your name for you while you are still alive, with total freedom to do with your property as he or she wants. It is *not* a plan for your family's protection. Even if it works and you give the person a list of instructions, you have no guarantees they will be followed. A power of attorney has benefits when used under proper circumstances, but it should not be used as a primary estate plan to avoid probate.

Summary

Now you know about the risks involved with the more common methods people use to try and avoid probate. A living trust has none of these risks. It completely avoids all probate and lets your plan stay your plan—it won't be altered by the court, unforeseen legal technicalities, or greedy relatives.

Before we explain how a living trust does all of this—and so you can fully appreciate its advantages—you need to understand what happens in probate and how it can affect you and your family. As we mentioned earlier, probate can happen in three instances—when you die, if you become incompetent and when minor children are involved. We'll take a look at each of these situations now. It probably won't be very exciting reading, but we've tried to keep it as interesting as possible. So, bear with us—it will be worth it in the end.

One general note—as we mentioned earlier in the introduction, our intent is to explain, in general and understandable terms, what can happen to you and your family in probate. There may be some slight differences in your state's probate laws, but generally these will only be technical in nature and won't affect the general process.

1 WHEN YOU DIE

Whether or not you have a will when you die, the process to probate your estate (your possessions and debts at the time of your death) is virtually the same. Your family will not be able to change titles on property still listed in your name without a court order—it can only be done through the probate court. This includes *any* titled property—bank accounts, real estate, car, etc. Even if you had a will, in most states a court order is required because a will by itself is not enough authority to retitle property or release account balances.

The Probate Process

1. First, Of Course, You Die.

Your executor (if you named one in your will) has not yet been formally appointed by the court and can take only limited actions at this point—such as notifying your employer and bank of your death, requesting cancellation of the utilities to your home, and canceling magazine and newspaper subscriptions. If you didn't have a will, a family member can take care of these things, but legally this is about all they can do at this time.

Your family and/or friends cannot legally take any of your belongings before the probate process has been completed, unless they get specific approval from the court. In fact, there could be serious consequences if they do. (You've probably seen or heard of relatives taking personal belongings and sentimental items immediately after the funeral. If it's your family, *don't do it.* And if you're named an executor, *don't let anyone do it.*) Several steps, which follow, must be taken before *any* property can be distributed to your heirs.

2. File Petition

Probate does not automatically happen upon your death. Someone must request that probate proceedings begin—usually when property needs to be sold, checks need to be written from your bank account, money withdrawn from an account, or when other assets need to be liquidated or transferred to a new owner.

Usually a family member (when there is no will) or your executor (when there is a will) will request that probate proceedings begin. This is a formal process. A written petition, prepared by an attorney, is submitted to the court to start the proceedings and will usually include your original will (if you had one). A filing fee (paid from your assets) will be charged to your estate, usually when the petition is presented to the court.

3. Publication

After the petition is filed, in most states the court will order a formal notice of your death published in a local newspaper for several weeks or months before the first hearing. This procedure notifies the public of your death, requests that your creditors present any unpaid debts to the court, and invites anyone who feels he or she has a right to part of your estate to come forward and make a claim. The cost of this advertising (usually several hundreds of dollars) is paid from the assets in your estate.

At the same time, your executor notifies your named heirs of your death, sends each of them a copy of your will (if you had one), and advises them where the probate proceedings will be held. This is when everyone finds out how much you left them—or didn't leave them.

4. First Hearing

The first hearing is usually held six weeks to two months after the filing of the petition. Assuming there are no contests of your will or any other unusual circumstances, the following steps usually occur at this hearing.

Will Is Validated

If you had a will, it must be validated by the court. The judge must make sure it meets the state's legal requirements—that it is the correct will (if you left more than one), that you were in a competent state of mind when it was drawn up, that all the proper signatures are on it, that it was witnessed, and so on. If your will is not accepted as valid, the judge will declare that you died without a will and will apply the state's will instead.

Executor/Administrator Is Appointed

After the will is validated (and "admitted" into probate), the court will formally appoint the executor (sometimes called a *personal representative*) to manage your estate for the court. If you had a will, you probably named someone to be your executor. If this person is still alive and able to act in this capacity, the judge will usually go along with your choice. If not, the judge will appoint someone else, usually a relative, sometimes an attorney or a bank's trust department.

If you did not have a will, the court will appoint an *administrator* to perform these duties. (An executor and an administrator have the same responsibilities. To help keep things simple, we will use the one term *executor* when referring to this position from now on.)

Probate is very slow—it can take years

Executor's Duties And Fees

The executor helps the court to inventory your possessions and determine their values. He/she is also responsible for collecting your bills and preparing your final tax returns, and for presenting them to the court to be approved and paid. The executor also applies to Social Security, veteran, union or fraternal organizations, and other groups or organizations for any death benefits to which your estate is entitled.

The court will grant your executor "letters testamentary." This is a legal document, an order signed by the judge, which formally appoints the executor, giving him/her the authority to act in your place under court supervision. These "letters" are what the bank and others need to close out your accounts and turn your assets over to your executor. In effect, the titles of your property transfer from you to your executor, who is responsible for their safekeeping while your estate is probated.

Executors are entitled to receive payment for their services and are often required to post a bond, both of which are normally paid from the assets in your estate.

It is important to remember that in many states the executor does not have the authority to act independently—every action is controlled and ultimately must be approved by the probate court. So, even though your estate is paying for his/her services, your executor is actually working for the court.

Independent Administration

Recently some states have adopted *independent administration,* in which the executor's actions and records are not audited or approved by the court. This does reduce the amount of paperwork, but the estate is still in probate and it's still a slow process. The requirements for independent administration vary in each state which permits it. In California, for example, the court can permit independent administration unless your will specifically states that you do not want it. In other states, you must specifically include in your will that you want your estate to be independently administered, or *all* of your beneficiaries must agree to give the executor this unsupervised authority. It may be difficult to get them all to agree, and can be especially so if they live far apart.

Unusual Circumstances

If your will is contested or if there are any other unusual circumstances, the court will try to resolve them at this first hearing. If the differences cannot be resolved at this time, there will be subsequent hearings until the conflict can be resolved by the court. The court will decide if anyone who claims to be one of your "heirs" has a valid right to part of your estate, whether or not you included him or her in your will. It is not uncommon for these "heirs" to find out how much your estate is worth from the newspaper publications and court files, and hire an attorney to contest the will—sometimes even when they have no real hope of getting anything. Because contesting a will can get very expensive and prolongs probate, families very often pay off contesting heirs just to get rid of them.

Also, since executors are entitled to be paid for their services, more than one of your relatives or friends may want this responsibility, resulting in additional court hearings to determine who finally will be appointed by the court. This can significantly increase the time and costs of probate, and could result in hurt feelings as well. Even if you specify an executor in your will, your choice can be contested.

File Opened/Attorney Appointed

At the end of the first hearing, the court will formally open a file on your estate and will usually appoint an attorney to handle the estate's paperwork for the court. Although having an attorney is not always a legal requirement, it has become a practical necessity because probate paperwork and filing procedures can be extremely complicated. Also, judges prefer to deal with attorneys who understand how the probate system works. If you did not specify an attorney in your will, your family may request a specific attorney or the court will select one. Of course, all attorney fees are paid from the assets in your estate.

5. Assets Frozen/Inventory Estate
During probate, your assets are usually frozen so that an accurate inventory of your property and possessions can be taken. This means that your heirs cannot receive their inheritances, nor can any property or assets be sold or liquidated without the court's permission.

Assets are usually frozen during probate

After the first hearing, the executor must locate all of your possessions and property, compile a list of them and their values, and present it to the court. This can be a very time-consuming and difficult process, especially if you (like most people) did not have current and accurate records, if you had assets in several states, etc. The court will usually require formal appraisals (usually by a certified, court-approved appraiser) for many items, such as real estate, antiques, collectibles, automobiles, furniture, etc. Appraisal fees can be expensive and are also paid from your estate.

Family Living Allowance
During this time, your dependents (spouse, minor children, and perhaps elderly parents) will probably be allowed a living allowance, but it must be "reasonable" and approved by the court. To request the allowance, your dependent(s) must submit a written request to the court through an attorney. If there are a number of outstanding debts, or if the will is being contested, a judge may insist that the assets remain intact and reduce—or even deny—the request.

However, proceeds from assets with beneficiary designations (such as life insurance, IRAs, retirement plans, etc.) are usually paid direct to your beneficiary without probate, so your family will probably have some money for living expenses. (However, if you have named "my estate" as your beneficiary, the proceeds must go through probate first. We'll discuss this more in Part Two.) Also, the court will usually allow your dependents to continue living in your home during probate, even if it will eventually go to someone else.

6. Presentation And Payment Of Debts, Claims And Taxes
Your creditors have a certain number of days from the first publication notice of your death to come forward and submit their claims against your estate for

payment. After this time has passed, the executor will audit the claims and present them to the court for approval to pay them from the assets in your estate. If there are any disputes over a claim, there could be additional hearings (at additional costs), with the judge ultimately making the final decision.

7. Final Distribution/Closing Of Estate

Finally, after the court is satisfied that the legal process has been completed—in most cases, at least a year or more later—it will usually order another publication to announce a final hearing to close your estate. At this hearing, the judge will review all the paperwork and order your debts, claims, taxes and probate expenses (including attorney and executor fees, probate fees, bonds and appraisals) paid.

The cash assets in an estate can be greatly reduced, even consumed, because of the ongoing expenses of probate. If there is not enough cash in your estate to pay your debts, the judge can order your property, including your personal belongings, sold at a public auction or estate sale. Many times this will be on a "distressed sale" basis or in a depressed market.

After all bills have been paid, the court will order your remaining property distributed to your heirs according to your will (or the state's will if you didn't have one). The judge will then order the executor relieved of his/her duties and the file closed.

8. Multiple Probate?

If you owned real estate in more than one state, this entire process (and its expenses) will probably have to be repeated in each state in which the real estate is located.

Exception—Very Small Estates

The only real exception to the process as we explain it here is that some states have a shortened probate process for *very small estates*. Estates that qualify can be probated without an attorney or executor fairly quickly and with just a minimum filing fee. But very few qualify for this special process, because the limits on the total estate value are usually extremely low—as low as $15,000 in some states.

What The Probate Process Does To Your Family

Probate can consume up to 10% or more of your estate's gross value

Probate Is Expensive

Before your heirs can receive *any* part of your estate, all expenses connected with the probate process must be paid. And there are a lot of them—filing fees and court costs, publication and advertising expenses, appraisal and auction costs, bond fees, and attorney and executor fees.

You should know that the probate judge does not directly take any of this money. Judges are paid to enforce the laws from our tax dollars. And, generally speaking, the government doesn't take money directly from your estate when you die, unless it is large enough to have to pay estate taxes. (These are also known as death taxes. We'll discuss them later in Part Three.)

Attorney And Executor Fees Are Hard To Predict

Usually the biggest expense of probate is attorney and executor fees, which can easily run into many thousands of dollars. Each state has its own method for determining these fees. Some states establish a guideline to help regulate fees, based on a percentage of the gross or net value of the estate. But a judge can (and often does) approve higher fees, based on individual circumstances and the time involved. Other states permit hourly fees—$75 to $200 per hour is not an unusual attorney rate. Usually the executor will receive a lower hourly rate, but some states specify that the executor will be paid the same rate as the attorney.

Most executors and attorneys are required by the court to keep a detailed record of the amount of time they spend on each case—telephone calls, letters, answering questions, court appearances, etc. Generally speaking, the more time they have to spend probating an estate, the more costly the probate process becomes.

So How Much Does Probate Cost?

On the average across the country, total probate costs are often estimated to be from 5% to 10% of an estate's *gross* value, which is the market value of an estate at death *before* any debts have been paid. In many states, probate fees are actually calculated on the gross estate value—that means if your home is valued at $100,000 when you die, probate fees will be calculated on the full $100,000, even if the mortgage is $80,000.

The following chart shows fees in California, Missouri and New York for just the attorney and executor. (California is about average for most states; yours may be higher or lower.) These figures do not include other probate costs such as filing and appraisal fees, bonds or publication fees, or legal fees if your will is contested.

Examples of Probate Fees

Estate Value	Combined Fees For Attorney and Executor*		
	California	*Missouri*	*New York*
$100,000	$6,300	$6,600	$10,000
$200,000	$10,300	$12,100	$18,000
$500,000	$22,300	$28,100	$38,000
$1,000,000	$42,300	$53,100	$68,000
$2,000,000	$62,300	$93,100	$118,000
$5,000,000	$122,300	$213,100	$268,000

*Minimum fees for California and Missouri; average fees in New York.

Probate costs can easily exceed the fee ranges given above. In fact, few estates are probated for just the minimum allowed fees—in many probates, the attorney and executor will usually request (and are granted) additional fees, especially if there are extenuating circumstances.

For example, if your will is contested or ruled invalid by the court, attorney fees and court costs can escalate dramatically. If you own several real estate properties which will need to be sold, the appraisal and publication costs will be more than if your estate has no real estate. If you die without a will, the court will have to spend more time determining your heirs (enforcing the state's will) and deciding who will be your administrator. If you die leaving small children, the court will have to establish a guardianship for them (which requires additional court hearings and testimony).

Every additional decision or transaction required to complete the probate process will increase the costs. It is virtually impossible to predict the final probate costs for any estate—there's just no way of knowing until the actual process has been fully completed.

But I Don't Have That Much. Why Should I Be Concerned About The Cost Of Probate?

Probate can affect *any* size estate, large or small, and especially those with any amount of real estate. Generally speaking, *probate costs take a greater percentage from smaller estates than larger ones.* And smaller estates just cannot afford to risk probate, because there isn't that much to go around to begin with. Find out the costs of probate in your state—you may be surprised how much it costs for even a modest estate, especially if real estate is involved.

The probate process, not your family, has control

But in addition to the financial costs, there are other, often immeasurable, costs of probate. We'll look at these now.

Your Family Loses Control

As we mentioned earlier, during probate your family may not be able to sell property or liquidate assets without court approval, even if they need the money. The probate process, not your family, has control—and your family must try to live their lives within the restrictions of the probate system. Families are used to dealing with their affairs privately and independently. Suddenly losing that control to a court *and* having to pay for the court to tell them who gets what and when can be very frustrating.

Probate Takes Time

Probate delays can also be extremely frustrating. Remember, the probate system must follow legal procedures exactly, and this process is notoriously slow. As we mentioned earlier, probate usually takes 1-2 years, often longer. Some of the time required for probate is very specific, such as how long the publication notices of your death must run in the papers (in those states that require it) and how long your creditors have to present their claims.

Other parts of the process are totally unpredictable. For example, your executor may need additional time to get your affairs in order and to locate all of your assets. Of course, any complications (such as if your will is contested) will create additional delays. John Wayne's will, as an example, was admitted to probate in 1979 and probate hearings were still being held as late as 1990.

Also, in reality, a good part of the time required for probate is due to the overbooked court system. Even if everything else runs smoothly, it may take several months to get a court date.

Probate files are public record

Time Is Money

Your assets can deteriorate while tied up in probate. Stocks, real estate and other assets can lose value if they cannot be sold quickly enough in a declining market. Your heirs could miss out on certain opportunities that require an immediate decision, such as a land development offering or stock transaction. Remember, probate is a slow process, and in today's financial world, these decisions must often be made quickly.

No Privacy

All probate proceedings are a matter of public record. In those states that require it, advertising allows your creditors to present their unpaid bills, but it also encourages the interest and attention of those who may feel they have a right to part of your estate (whether or not they actually do). You may have purposely left out some of your heirs in your will, but they can contest your will and the court—not you or your family—will decide if they are entitled to receive a share of your estate. Remember how many people claimed to be somehow "related" to Howard Hughes when he died?

Since it is public record, anyone can go to the probate court and find out details of your estate. It's surprising how easy it actually is—usually all you need to know is the name of the person and the year in which he or she died.

For example, a perfect stranger can look up actress Natalie Wood's file and see all the details of her almost $6 million estate—including her interest in the television series *Charlie's Angels* (valued at $2.3 million); royalties from movies; investments in real estate, oil and gas leases; artwork; a yacht; at least nine separate bank accounts. It's amazing how detailed the records are—even her half of an $83.31 refund from the telephone company is included in her assets. You can also see exactly how much she left her mother, sisters, daughters and husband—and their addresses at the time of her death.

In Vic Morrow's file (the famous actor who was tragically killed while filming the television series *The Twilight Zone*), you can read his handwritten will in which he practically disinherited one daughter (leaving her only $100), left his good friend $50,000 and left the rest of his $1 million estate (including his dog *Macho*) to his other daughter.

In Nat King Cole's probate file, you can read that the famous singer was so heavily in debt that only about $350,000 of his almost $2 million estate went to his heirs. He was also ill for some time before he died—and his file contains correspondence regarding disputes over his medical expenses.

Obviously, probate files can make for some pretty interesting reading for the curious (or nosy). Our point is this: would you want *anyone* to be able to find out what *you* owned—and owed?

Devastating To A Business Owner

Now you may not be as wealthy as these famous people were, but if you are a business owner, lack of privacy could be disastrous to your business. Private financial records and personal family affairs become public information, and anyone can have access to them. Your competitor(s) can have valuable "inside information"—courtesy of the probate court.

Exposes Your Family To Unscrupulous Solicitors

Some people think, "I won't be around then anyway, so why should I care who sees what I've got?" Maybe you've even thought this yourself. Well, the truth is that you *should* care—maybe not for yourself, but for those you leave behind. If you make your loved ones go through probate, you could be exposing them to possible exploitation.

There are people who go through probate records and compile lists of new widows and beneficiaries. These lists are then sold as leads to those selling "investments," offering to "manage" finances, or other "helpful" activities. Some of these are legitimate, but many are outright scams—unscrupulous solicitors who prey upon bereaved survivors, especially spouses, who are at a particularly vulnerable time in their lives. Many of these surviving spouses have never had to handle finances before and are not only emotionally upset about the loss of their partners, but are understandably terrified about being alone and on their own.

Emotional Costs

Because it is an ongoing process, probate can be a frequent interruption, preventing your family from resuming their own lives and serving as a constant reminder of your absence. It can also cause unpleasant disagreements among family members who would normally look to one another for support.

A family is used to running its own affairs in private, according to its needs. You make decisions on a daily, even hourly, basis to accommodate different situations and personalities. But probate rules and regulations are very rigid, and the law cannot bend or make allowances for individuals. When it seems that nothing is happening, or that things are taking too long to resolve, it's often impossible for a family member to get answers. The court will not directly communicate with the family (a judge's duty is to enforce the law, not to give legal advice), so all communication regarding the estate must go through an attorney.

It's easy for family and in-laws to become frustrated, and because they cannot take out their frustrations on the court, they may end up taking them out on each other. When people react emotionally instead of rationally, it's often impossible to reach an agreement, and the court may have to get involved to settle what should have been a simple agreement worked out among caring family members.

It's Your Choice—But There's More!

Even if you don't think you need a living trust to transfer your property when you die, you may want to read a little further—because we're not through yet. Would you believe that probate can take control while you are still alive?

2 IF YOU BECOME PHYSICALLY OR MENTALLY INCAPACITATED

Most people usually associate probate with "something that happens when you die." Few know that the probate court can take control of your financial and personal affairs *before* you die—and even fewer plan for this possibility.

But if you become physically or mentally incapacitated and are no longer able to handle your own personal and financial affairs, you will most likely be declared incompetent and placed under the control of the probate court in something called a *conservatorship* (also called a *probate guardianship* in some states)—even if you have a will, and especially if you own any titled property (home, other real estate, car, bank/savings accounts, etc.).

A Growing Concern Of Millions

Your will can't help if you become incompetent

Becoming physically or mentally incapacitated and losing control of their lives is a valid concern of millions of older Americans—and those who will care for them. With advances in modern medicine, people are living longer. But this also means that many of us will reach the point where we can no longer take care of ourselves, becoming incapacitated for some time before we die. Unless we plan now, a conservatorship is a very real possibility.

But not just older people end up in conservatorships. It can happen to any of us, at any time—and at any age. Without warning, you could be critically injured in an accident or stricken with a devastating illness (physical or mental) and be left alive, but without the capacity to handle your own affairs.

Why A Will Won't Protect You

Some people think that if they have a will, their spouse, parent or adult child (or whomever they have named as executor in their will) can automatically step in and take care of their day-to-day affairs if they should become incapacitated. But a will can only go into effect *after* you die. It cannot help if you become physically or mentally incapacitated—because you're still alive.

What Is A Conservatorship?

This is a legal process that was created to protect you and your property if you are unable to take care of your own affairs. The original intention was, of course, very honorable. To prevent someone from taking over your property and squandering your possessions, the court will step in and take control, making financial decisions for you and looking after your welfare.

What's Wrong With It?

Most people would prefer that a family member or friend take care of them, not the court. But if you are placed in a conservatorship, the court takes over—and you and your family lose all direct control. You lose most of your legal rights, and you have no choice about how your money is spent or who will look after your care. Even if a family member is named as your conservator (called a guardian in some states), the court will still control your money. And, just like probate at death, a conservatorship is expensive and time consuming.

If you can't sign your name, only the probate court can sign for you

Why The Probate Court Will Get Involved

If you own titled property (home, other real estate, car, bank/savings accounts, etc.) in just your name and you are no longer able to sign your name because you are mentally or physically incapacitated, someone will eventually have to ask the court to step in and act for you.

Now, let's think about this for just a moment. Sooner or later, your signature will probably be required for something—to withdraw savings, sell or refinance property or other assets to pay your expenses, etc. But your spouse, family or friends *cannot* sign your name for you if yours is the only authorized signature—the court must do it for you through a conservatorship. And if any of your titled property must be sold for any reason, including to pay for your care, only the probate court can sign your name to transfer the title.

Of course, you may still be able to physically sign your name but, in the opinion of others, are unable to make sound decisions. If the court agrees, you will be declared incompetent and placed in a conservatorship.

Joint Ownership Often Causes A Conservatorship

If you own titled property jointly (especially real estate) and one of the joint owners becomes physically or mentally incapacitated, the other cannot sell or refinance the property without court involvement—even if your joint owner is your spouse. This is because *both* signatures are required to transfer title, and if one of the owners cannot sign his/her name, *only the court* can sign for that owner. So, in effect, you'll find yourself with a *new* joint owner—*the probate court*. And once the court gets involved, it stays involved until that person recovers or dies.

Many people are surprised to learn this. That's because they mistakenly think joint ownership of property works just like a joint bank account. But they are *very* different. A joint bank account is actually a contract with the bank that allows each joint "owner" to independently make deposits, withdrawals, even close the account. Joint ownership *of property* (stocks, bonds, real estate, etc.) is something altogether different. To transact any business (buy, sell, get a loan, refinance, etc.) requires the signatures of *all* of the owners. *One owner cannot act for another*. It's understandable why people get confused. Just remember you do *not* have the same flexibility with joint ownership of property as you do with a joint banking account.

Here's an example of what can happen with joint ownership when one of the owners becomes incapacitated:

> Bill and Karen, a young professional couple in their 30's, were successful and responsible adults. They made safe investments and planned carefully for their future. They owned everything jointly and even had wills, leaving everything to each other. But in just seconds their lives changed dramatically—Bill was critically injured in a car accident.
>
> Karen could continue to sign checks and pay their day-to-day bills because only one of their signatures was required on their joint checking account. But soon the cash started running out, and Karen realized she needed to sell some of their investments, and maybe their house, to pay for Bill's care and the other bills. Karen found that she was unable to sell any of their jointly owned property without both signatures. Since Bill could no longer sign his name, the only way Karen could sell their property was to place Bill into a conservatorship and have the court sign *for* him. Bill's will was no help at all because he was still alive.
>
> Karen had no idea how expensive and cumbersome this process would be. Not only did she have to deal with Bill's situation and the effect of this tragedy on their personal lives, but now she also had to deal with the restrictions of the court system. The court had to approve everything—the sale of their jointly owned property and how Bill's share of that money was spent, even though it was used to pay their personal bills and take care of Bill. When Bill died several years later, Karen found herself back in probate court—this time to probate his will.

The Conservatorship Process

Generally, this is what happens if you are placed in a conservatorship. Some steps, as you will see, are very similar to the probate process at death. But keep in mind that while this process is going on, you are still alive.

1. Petition The Court

The court must be petitioned by someone on your behalf to begin proceedings to determine if you are incompetent. Usually a relative or neighbor will hire an attorney to start these proceedings. Very often, because of your condition, you will not know anything about this. In fact, some states do not even require that you be told.

2. Proceedings Advertised

In most states, a notice of the proceedings will be advertised in the local papers to allow your creditors a chance to present any unpaid bills to the court. This also makes your situation public.

3. Competency Hearing

A hearing is held to determine your competency. In some states, you are not even required to be present and the judge bases his/her decision on reports and testimony. If the probate judge decides that you are incompetent, you immediately lose most of your individual rights as a citizen.

4. Conservator/Attorney Appointed

The judge will appoint a conservator to handle your affairs for you (pay your bills, etc.) and make sure you receive proper care. Usually the conservator is a relative, but the judge can appoint anyone to this position, even someone you would not have wanted to take care of you. A conservatorship file is opened on you, and is available to the public. Conservators are entitled to be paid for their services and are required to post a bond. The court will also appoint an attorney to take care of the required paperwork.

5. Inventory Assets And Debts

The conservator makes a list of your assets and debts and submits them, along with a budget for your living expenses, to the court for approval. The court may order your property and personal belongings sold at public auction to help pay your expenses, including the costs of the conservatorship.

6. The Court Takes Control—Or Does It?

From this point, all of your affairs are handled by your court-appointed conservator, under the direct supervision of the court. Depending on the court system, your conservator may have to deal with a very strict monitoring system—or one with very little control.

If the court is very strict, all expenditures your conservator makes on your behalf (including medical care and even personal items, right down to toothpaste) must be documented and approved by the court, creating a lot of paperwork. Once a year, the attorney must submit a report of every financial transaction. This report is audited and must be approved by the court, and it often takes months to complete the process.

The court, not your family, makes decisions for you

Other courts are not strict at all, usually because they do not have the resources to properly monitor the financial records. In these situations, the assets can (and often do) simply disappear without a trace—with no record of how the money was spent.

7. Ending A Conservatorship

It is very difficult and expensive to end a conservatorship (usually it will continue until the person dies). If you recover and are once again able to take care of yourself, you must petition the court and prove your competency. You must hire an attorney to represent you, and you will probably have to hire at least one trained professional (psychiatrist, psychologist, etc.) to confirm that you are now "well" and able to take care of yourself. Practically speaking, this could be difficult, if not impossible, to do. (You may have a hard time convincing an attorney, doctors and judge that you are now competent when a court has already declared you *in*competent.)

8. Probate Again

When you die, your family will have to go through probate all over again—this time to distribute your remaining assets to your heirs. A conservatorship only exists while you are alive—it does not replace probate when you die. So, after your conservatorship file is closed (sometimes many months after your death), your remaining assets will be transferred to another court file and the formal process we discussed earlier will begin.

How A Conservatorship Affects You And Your Family

Because a conservatorship is conducted by the probate court, you and your family will be affected in many of the same ways as when an estate is probated at death. The process is still inflexible, expensive, and time consuming, but a conservatorship can go on indefinitely—until you either recover or die.

You And Your Family Lose Control

The court, not your family, basically makes all decisions for you—appointing your conservator, approving how your money is spent and deciding the

Most families want to handle these matters privately

quality of your care. Even if someone in your family is appointed your conservator, the court will audit the financial records.

Takes Time

Since the court has to approve your expenses, this takes more time than if you are cared for *outside* the court system. Besides making sure you receive proper care, your conservator will have to spend additional time keeping up with the paperwork and satisfying the court's requirements. This could be especially hard for an elderly spouse to handle if he/she is appointed as your conservator.

No Privacy

All probate proceedings are matters of public record. Your personal and financial information is available for anyone to see (and remember, you're still alive). You may not want this information (and your condition) being made public—especially if you are a business owner or are active (and known) in your community.

Emotional Costs

This can be a very difficult time for your family. It's hard enough for most families to adjust to the reality of this kind of situation, and usually they want to take care of these matters *privately*. The conservatorship process can only add to their frustration. And, if the court orders your possessions sold at public auction to pay for your expenses, it could be an added emotional strain for your family to have to publicly sell your possessions while you are still alive.

Financial Costs

All costs associated with your conservatorship—filing fees, conservatorship fees and bonds, advertising, appraisals, and attorney fees—are paid from your assets. The costs are unpredictable and can easily add up, especially if you require complicated medical care, have a lot of assets to manage or other special needs, and if the conservatorship continues for years. The additional expense of a conservatorship can be especially hard on an older couple living on a fixed income.

Don't forget the hidden costs. Your assets cannot be sold without the permission of the court, and real estate, stocks and other investments can quickly lose value while they are tied up in probate.

Conservator Battles

The court must appoint your conservator, which can lead to a long and expensive court battle if, for whatever reason, more than one person wants this position. Remember the Groucho Marx competency hearings, in which a woman friend of his tried to convince the court that he wanted her as his conservator? Although Groucho was living with this woman at the time and she had been taking care of him, the court eventually appointed a relative as his conservator. The hearings were lengthy, expensive, very public and probably taxing on Groucho (he died shortly after the hearings ended)—not a very pleasant situation for any family to risk having to go through.

Potential For Abuse

As in Groucho's case, the court will usually appoint a family member as your conservator. But if you are alone and have no trusted relatives who live nearby, a scheming relative, associate or neighbor may find it very appealing to have you declared incompetent, have himself or herself appointed as your conservator, put you into a nursing home and take control of your assets. (Remember, the court may not even require you to be at the competency hearing.)

And, as we mentioned earlier, you run the risk of being placed under the protection of a court that does not have the resources to properly monitor your conservatorship—leaving the door wide open to possible abuse.

Again, You Have A Choice

You can risk being placed in a conservatorship. Or you can get a living trust, and keep control of your personal affairs—*privately*—even if you become physically or mentally incapacitated.

There is one more area in which probate can interfere with our lives, and that's when a minor child inherits money or property. If you have minor children or grandchildren, this section will be especially important to you. We'll briefly explain this next before we move on to living trusts.

3 MINOR CHILDREN AND PROBATE

When most people think about a court guardianship for a child, they think of a situation right out of a Charles Dickens novel, with the poor orphan caught between the lawyers, the court and the guardian. That's not so far off, even today.

But did you know that a child can be placed in a probate guardianship even when one or both parents are still alive? Minor children cannot legally transfer titles of property in their own names. So if a minor child inherits titled property (including real estate, stocks, bonds, etc.), is due to receive beneficiary proceeds (life insurance, IRA, etc.) or becomes a joint owner of property, the court will have to get involved at some point to protect the child's interests.

That's because only the court can sign for the child. Usually the court will get involved when the property needs to be sold or refinanced, but sometimes this happens even before the child can receive the money or be listed on the title, depending on the value and type of property.

These situations are not at all unusual, as we'll explain in just a moment.

How Children Can Be Placed In Probate Guardianships

If Both Parents Die

Of course, this is the most obvious situation, but there are some issues here which might surprise you. Most parents think that if they name a guardian for their minor children in their will, that person will automatically be able to step in at their death(s) and raise the child using the child's inheritance. But this is not what happens.

When your estate goes into probate after your death, the court must *appoint* a guardian for your child. If you name a guardian in your will, the court will usually go along with your choice to *raise* your child—but it doesn't have to. The court may appoint someone else if it decides that person would be better than your choice. (Of course, if you don't have a will, the court will make its decision without knowing your wishes.)

But—*and this is very important*—the *court*, not the guardian, will keep control over the child's inheritance through a probate guardianship. The guardian will have custody of the child, *but the court will have control of the money.*

The court, not the guardian, controls your child's inheritance

Problems With A Children's Trust In A Will

Some people put a children's trust in their will to prevent the court from taking control of the inheritance. But it probably doesn't work the way most people think—and it may not work at all when your children really need it.

First—because it is part of your will, the children's trust can only go into effect *after* your will has been probated. It is funded with your assets. Those with beneficiary designations (such as life insurance, IRAs, retirement plans, etc.) can be paid to your children's trust right away without probate *if* you have named your children's trust as the beneficiary. But other titled assets (including any real estate) will have to be probated *first*—and that takes time, costs money, etc. (you know the story by now). So it could be months or years before these assets can get into your children's trust—minus, of course, the cost of probate. That could be "too little, too late" to provide for your children the way you had planned.

Second—what happens if you become physically or mentally incapacitated due to an illness or accident? You are still alive so your will can't be probated and the children's trust can't even go into effect. Plus, no beneficiary proceeds can be paid—because no one has died. And if both parents are incapacitated or if you are a single parent, the parent(s) *and* child will probably end up in a court conservatorship/guardianship.

If One Or Both Parents Are Still Living

We just explained that a guardianship may be required if one or both parents become incapacitated. You may be surprised to learn how relatives with good intentions can cause a guardianship even while one or both parents are still alive and healthy.

Inheriting

Many grandparents and other relatives (aunts, uncles, etc.) leave money, real estate, stocks, certificates of deposit (CDs), and other investments directly to a minor child (as do many parents). If the child is still a minor when the person dies and the estate is probated, the court will have to get involved, especially if the inheritance is substantial.

The court has to make sure the child's interests are "protected," even if both parents are alive and well. Of course, this protection isn't free, and the child's inheritance (or the parents) will have to pay for it. An attorney will need to represent the child in court and the court will probably insist that a guardian (usually a parent) is added to the titles when they are transferred to the child.

Establishing the guardianship is a relatively simple process, but once it is in place the court will stay involved. Until the child reaches legal age, none of the properties can be sold (or the money spent) without the court's approval. And this guardianship could go on indefinitely if the child is physically or mentally incapacitated when he/she reaches legal age.

Minor Children As Beneficiaries

Here's something else you may not have known. Most life insurance companies will not knowingly pay these benefits directly to a minor child—nor will they pay to another person *for* the child (such as to a parent)—and will usually require proof of a court approved guardianship. They just do not want the potential legal liabilities. This also applies to other assets you have which permit beneficiary designations, such as your IRA, retirement plans, etc.

Many people are not aware of this and list their minor children or grandchildren as beneficiaries (either primary or secondary) on their life insurance policies and other accounts without realizing the risk.

Joint Ownership With A Minor

You do not want to list a minor as a joint owner of any titled property—including real estate, automobile, boat, stocks, etc.—because the only way to sell or refinance the property later is through a court guardianship. Here's another case of good intentions with devastating consequences:

> Stella, who was recently divorced, added her 12-year old son as joint owner on the deed to her house, thinking it would automatically become his if she should die suddenly. A year later, she needed to sell the house. But she couldn't, because her 13-year old son (her joint owner) could not legally sign the papers. She had to put her own son in a probate

guardianship and the court insisted on approving the sale. By that time, the buyers were long gone—but the court was still there. Eventually she was able to find another buyer, and this time the sale went through. But the court kept control over her son's share of the proceeds until he turned 18—at which time he promptly spent it all on a sports car, a motorcycle and "good times." In the meantime, Stella couldn't afford to buy another house with just her share. She found out the hard way that joint ownership with a minor does not work.

Your child can get caught in the middle

Simply put, if you leave any titled property directly to your minor children or grandchildren, *or* make a child a joint owner, *or* list a child as a beneficiary on your life insurance, IRA, retirement benefits, etc., you could unknowingly be setting up a probate guardianship for the child.

The Guardianship Process

A probate guardianship for minor children works basically the same way as for adults who cannot handle their own affairs and have been declared incompetent. The child's court-appointed guardian will need to hire an attorney, post bond and submit a report to the court each year. Anything the child needs that costs money (including education, school and social activities, music lessons, clothes, etc.) must be submitted in a written request by the attorney and approved by the court. And, of course, the guardianship costs money, which comes from the child's inheritance.

Besides the financial costs, there can also be *emotional* costs. Guardians and the court can get into disagreements over what is and is not important for the child's welfare. For instance, the guardian may feel it is very important for the child's development to take music lessons or to attend certain social functions—while the court may feel these expenditures are unnecessary, or even frivolous. And the child is caught in the middle (shades of Charles Dickens). How do you explain all of this to a child?

This guardianship will continue until the minor child legally becomes an adult at age 18 (or 21, depending on the state in which you live). At this time, the child will automatically have *full control* over all of the inheritance. Many parents do not feel their children are mature enough at this age to handle this financial responsibility, and would prefer that they inherit at a later age or in installments (receiving some money at age 21, more at 25, etc.). But a court guardianship can't continue after a child has reached the legal age in that state.

Remember, too, if the court is not able to properly monitor the guardianship and the wrong person is appointed guardian, the child's inheritance could disappear—this does happen. An understaffed or lax court could be a real incentive for someone to *pretend* he or she is concerned about the child just to be named guardian—when all that person is *really* concerned about is the child's money.

How A Probate Guardianship Affects Your Child And Your Family

You Lose Control

The court, not the guardian you named in your will, controls your child's inheritance. The court can also override your choice of guardian and appoint someone else to raise your child. And your child will receive the entire inheritance when he/she legally becomes an adult in your state—you have no alternative.

A children's trust in a will does prevent the court from taking control of the inheritance and lets you leave specific instructions for how the money will be spent, when your child will inherit, etc. But remember, the will *must* be probated first, and this can't happen if you are incapacitated.

Takes Time

Besides the time it takes to raise your child, the guardian will have to spend additional time dealing with the court—keeping accurate records, meeting with the attorney and satisfying the court's requirements. This additional responsibility can cause even the most sincere and conscientious guardian to make compromises. It may be easier to "stick to basics" that don't require more time and paperwork, than to put forth the extra effort required to get court approval for a child's special needs. And it is not unusual for this complicated process to cause the guardian to feel some resentment toward the child.

It also takes time for a court and attorney to react, so there is little flexibility and spontaneity when it comes to your child's needs.

No Privacy

Remember, all probate proceedings are public record, so anyone can find out the value of your child's inheritance and how it is being spent.

Emotional Costs
Within a family, each child is recognized as a unique individual with his/her own identity and needs. But, under the law, the court must treat everyone equally, making it difficult for the court to make exceptions and address the special needs of different children. Also, any disputes between the guardian, attorney and court could have a strong impact on a child who has already lost his or her parents.

The cost of the guardianship is paid from your child's inheritance

Financial Costs
All costs associated with the guardianship are paid from the child's inheritance. Since raising a child can present any number of special circumstances, these costs are unpredictable and will vary for each individual case. And, depending on the amount of the inheritance and the duration (and cost) of the guardianship, the child's inheritance may be greatly reduced by the time the child receives it.

A Special Note To Divorced Or Separated Parents:
If your child's other natural parent is living at the time of your death or incapacity, the court will probably appoint him/her as your child's guardian, even though you may have preferred someone else. Guardians are entitled to be paid for their services (from your child's inheritance) and this may be an incentive for your "ex" to be interested. In addition, if the court does not monitor the guardianship carefully, you run the risk of your "ex" having access to money that is intended to be used only for your child's welfare.

You Have A Choice Here, Too
You can do nothing, you can have a will, and you can even have a will with a children's trust in it—but you still risk having a probate guardianship for your minor children or grandchildren. A living trust will let you provide for them, and *make sure* the court does *not* get involved—even if you become incapacitated.

So, THAT'S PROBATE!

That may not have been the most exciting reading you've ever done. But we hope you understand why we wanted you to know about probate, and how it can take control when you die, if you become physically or mentally incapacitated, or if you have minor children or grandchildren—and how it can affect you and your family whether you are married or single, old or young.

If the risks don't bother you, or if you really don't care about what probate can do, then that's okay. You can still rely on a will (yours or the state's) or joint ownership to transfer your property at your death—or you can give it all away while you are living. At least now you know the risks (and the costs)—*before* your family unexpectedly gets caught in the middle of probate.

But if you want to completely avoid probate, keep reading. Now we can tell you all about a living trust—what it is, how it works, how it avoids probate—and how your living trust can keep you and your family from unnecessary financial and emotional hardship.

Part Two

THE LIVING TRUST ALTERNATIVE

Part Two— THE LIVING TRUST ALTERNATIVE

With a living trust you can completely avoid probate—when you die, if you become incompetent *and* when minor children are involved.

WHAT IS A LIVING TRUST AND HOW DOES IT AVOID PROBATE?

A living trust is a legal document that allows you to transfer ownership of your titled property (home, other real estate, car, checking/savings accounts, etc.) and your personal property (clothes, furniture, etc.) from your individual name to something called a "trust," which *you* control. Think of it as forming your own company, with you and your spouse as the only employees. You personally don't own your property anymore because everything is now owned by your new company (your trust). But you still have complete control over it.

Remember when we said there are only two ways to avoid probate—own nothing in your own name or have a living trust? A living trust lets you own nothing in *your* name, yet have complete control over everything in your *trust's* name. *Nothing changes except the names on the titles.* You continue to control everything just as you did before. Although it is simply a legal technicality, *this* is what keeps you and your family out of probate. Since you no longer own anything in your own name, there is nothing to probate when you die or if you become incompetent.

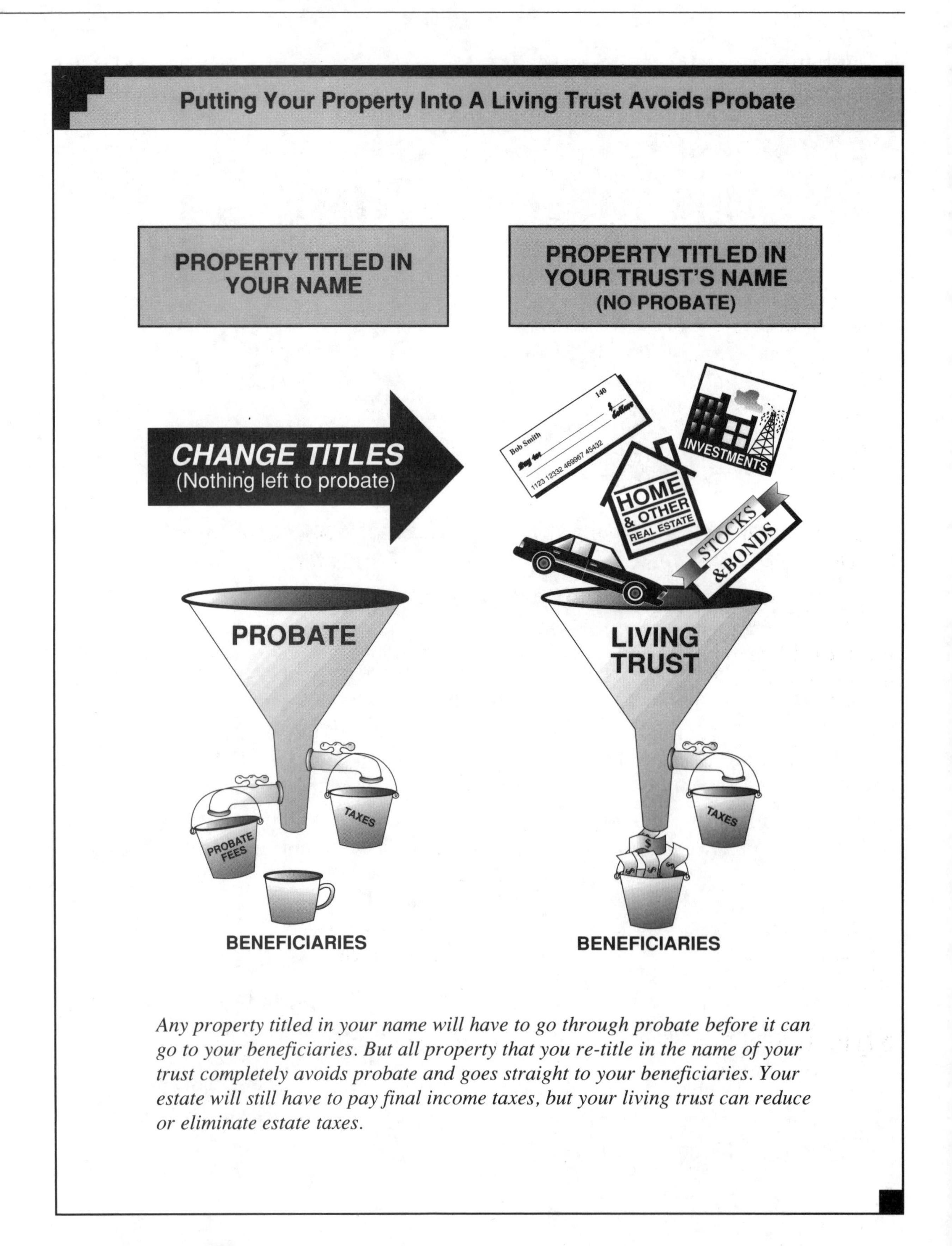

Any property titled in your name will have to go through probate before it can go to your beneficiaries. But all property that you re-title in the name of your trust completely avoids probate and goes straight to your beneficiaries. Your estate will still have to pay final income taxes, but your living trust can reduce or eliminate estate taxes.

A living trust avoids all probate

Living trusts are not new and they are not tax shelters or gimmicks. They do not need to be complicated or expensive. And they should be used by just about everyone. Married or single, old or young, whether your estate is modest or large—practically everyone can benefit from a living trust, especially if you have children or grandchildren (even more so if you are a single parent) or own any titled property.

If you want to make sure your loved ones (spouse, children *or* parents) will be spared from probate if something happens to you, you should have a living trust. Just ask any experienced bank or trust officer, investment broker, attorney, financial advisor, CPA or life insurance agent. Or ask a history teacher.

A Little History

Living trusts have been used successfully, in one form or another, for hundreds of years and, in fact, go back at least to the Middle Ages. The concept was used by knights who received land in exchange for providing services to the king (this usually meant going off to fight wars). To keep the land, the knight had to keep providing his services. After years of fighting the king's wars (and with the increasing availability of money taking the place of the barter system), the weary knight started paying the king a fee instead, and the king would then hire a mercenary to fight in the knight's place.

Eventually the knights got pretty smart and figured out that they could transfer the *title* of their land to the church (which was exempt from paying fees to the king), but retain the *use* of the land for their lifetimes or for several generations to come. This became known as a *trust*, because the knight *trusted* the church to allow him to continue *using* the land. So the knight kept the use of his land, the church got title to it, and the king didn't get his fees. This was the beginning of the living trust concept as we know it today. (Now, wasn't that interesting?)

Back To Modern Times

Today, instead of giving title of your property to the church, you give it to your trust. The legal name for a living trust is a *revocable inter vivos trust. Inter vivos* means that it is created while you are alive. *Revocable* means that it can be revoked or changed, even discontinued, by you at any time.

A living trust looks a lot like a will. In fact, it actually does what many people think a will does—it lets your property be distributed to the people or

You select the members of your living trust team

organizations you specify—but it does *not* go through probate. And it does a lot more, as we'll explain in this section.

HOW A LIVING TRUST WORKS

Your Living Trust Team

To understand how a living trust works, you need to understand the roles of the people involved with your trust and their legal names. The accompanying *Living Trust Team* chart will also be helpful.

The Grantor

When you set up your trust, you become what is called in legal terms the *grantor* (also called *creator, settlor* or *trustor*). This is the person *creating* the trust—you. If you and your spouse set up one trust together, you are both grantors of your trust.

The Trustee

You will name a *trustee* to manage the assets in your trust. This can be anyone you wish, including yourself. If you are your own trustee, you will continue to handle your affairs for as long as you are able. If you are married, you and your spouse can be *co-trustees*. This way, either of you can automatically act for the other (just like a joint checking account) and, if one of you becomes incompetent or dies, the other *instantly* has control of all trust property—*with no court involvement*. Remember, with a living trust, technically *neither* of you owns the property—your *trust* does. And, as co-trustees, *each* of you has the legal authority to act as trustee.

You don't have to be your own trustee if you don't want to or don't feel you are capable. There are many qualified institutions which manage trusts professionally (these are called corporate trustees), or you can name another individual (such as an adult son or daughter). In Part Four, we'll discuss these options in more detail.

The Back-Up Trustee

You will also need to name someone you know and trust as your *back-up trustee* (also called *successor trustee*) if you are the only trustee, or in case something happens to both you and your co-trustee. In order to step in and

Your Living Trust Team

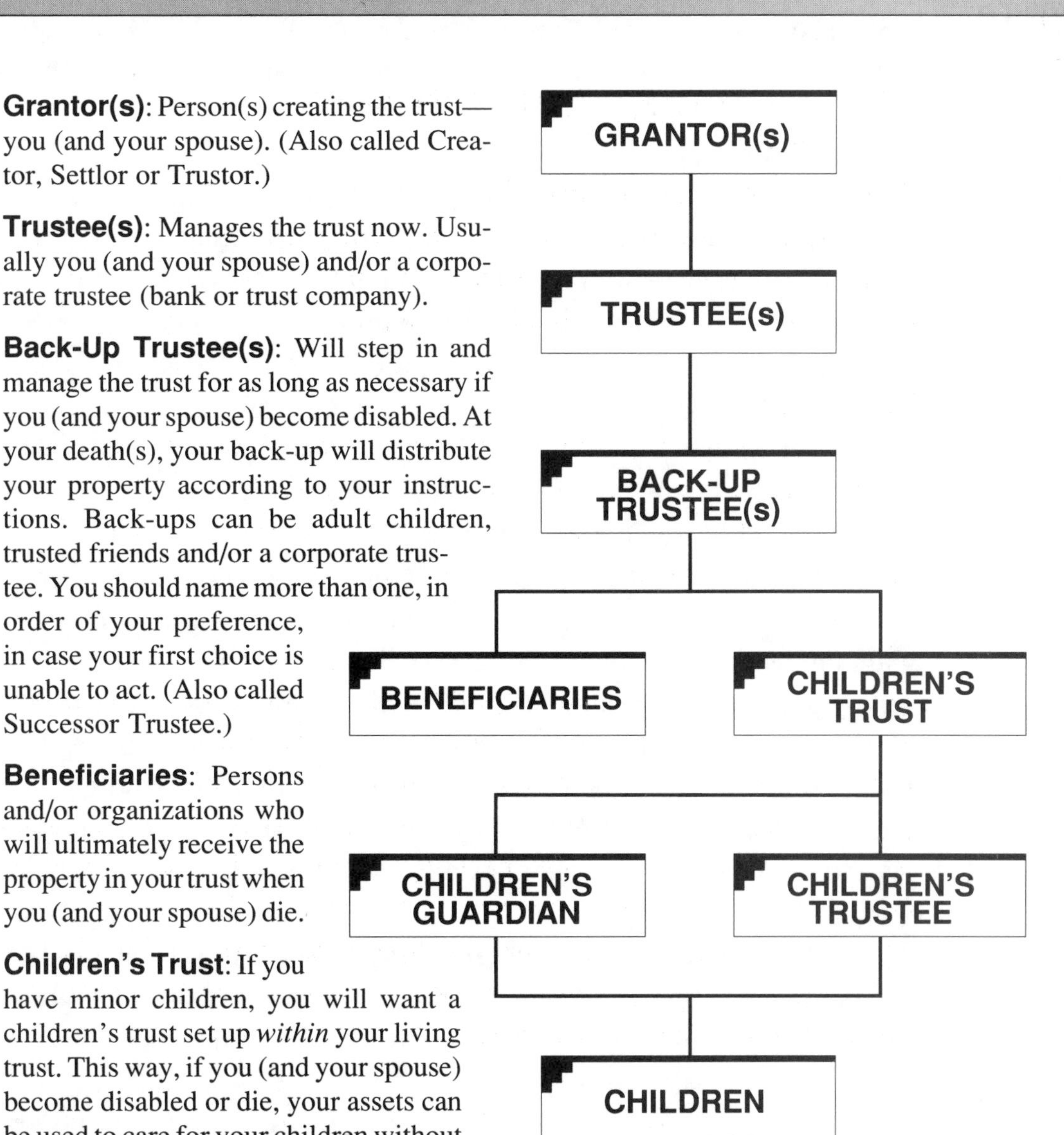

Grantor(s): Person(s) creating the trust—you (and your spouse). (Also called Creator, Settlor or Trustor.)

Trustee(s): Manages the trust now. Usually you (and your spouse) and/or a corporate trustee (bank or trust company).

Back-Up Trustee(s): Will step in and manage the trust for as long as necessary if you (and your spouse) become disabled. At your death(s), your back-up will distribute your property according to your instructions. Back-ups can be adult children, trusted friends and/or a corporate trustee. You should name more than one, in order of your preference, in case your first choice is unable to act. (Also called Successor Trustee.)

Beneficiaries: Persons and/or organizations who will ultimately receive the property in your trust when you (and your spouse) die.

Children's Trust: If you have minor children, you will want a children's trust set up *within* your living trust. This way, if you (and your spouse) become disabled or die, your assets can be used to care for your children without probate.

Guardian: Person you have named to raise your children if you (and your spouse) can't due to disability or death. Must be an adult.

Children's Trustee: Manages the assets in your children's trust until they reach the age(s) you specify they will inherit. Provides for education, maintenance, and support of your children from the assets in the trust. Can be the same person you name as guardian, another adult, and/or a corporate trustee.

... up trustee steps in for you when needed— with no court involvement

carry out your instructions, your back-up trustee will only need a copy of your death certificate (or a letter from your personal physician if you are incompetent), a copy of your trust document and personal identification to verify that he/she is the person you named to be trustee in your place.

The Beneficiaries

In a living trust, the people and/or organizations who will receive your property and possessions when you die are called your beneficiaries. Most people leave their property to relatives, but you can leave it to anyone or to any organization(s) you wish—many people like to include a favorite charity, foundation, religious or fraternal organization. You will also need to name an alternate beneficiary(ies) in case your primary ones do not survive you.

What Happens When You Die

Your back-up trustee (or co-trustee) will basically act as an executor would if you had a will—but does *not* have to report to the court. He/she pays your final bills (signing checks now as the trustee for your trust) and then follows your instructions for distributing your assets to your *beneficiaries*—even selling property, if that's what you wanted. Since all of your property is titled in the name of your trust, it's very easy for your back-up trustee to conduct business. The process is much quicker, less expensive and more private than probate. Your assets are *not* frozen and nothing is advertised, so no "heirs" are invited to make claims on your estate.

What Happens If You Become Incompetent

Your back-up trustee (or co-trustee) automatically steps in and handles your financial affairs for you. He/she can write checks, make deposits, apply for disability benefits, pay bills, sell property—anything necessary to keep your financial and personal affairs in order. No courts, attorneys or conservatorships are required, and everything is done privately. You and your family are spared the entire frustrating, time consuming and expensive process of having to set up a conservatorship and get the probate court's approvals to spend your own money.

Plus, you have peace of mind knowing that, if this should ever happen to you or your spouse, you will be taken care of by someone *you* have selected, someone you know and trust—not someone a court appoints to take care of you. If you recover, you simply start handling your affairs again and your

back-up trustee returns to being your back-up. There is no complicated paperwork or procedure to regain control.

Why You Can Be Sure Your Back-Up Trustee Will Follow Your Instructions

A living trust does give a lot of power to your back-up trustee. However, most properly prepared living trusts state that when your back-up trustee steps in for you and becomes your *acting* trustee, he/she must keep all of your other back-ups and beneficiaries informed of all actions. This way there are a lot of "checks" on your acting trustee's decisions.

In addition, a trust is a *binding legal contract* (unlike a will, which is simply a statement of your wishes and is only effective at death). Trustees are *fiduciaries*—by law they have a legal duty to follow your trust instructions and act in a *prudent* (conservative) manner at all times for the benefit of the trust beneficiaries. Obviously your back-up trustee(s) should be someone you can trust, but if your acting trustee were to "abuse" his/her fiduciary duties (by failing to follow the instructions in your trust document), he/she could be held legally liable.

In other words, while your acting trustee has broad powers, he/she always has a legal duty to carry out your instructions. This is very different from just giving someone a general "power of attorney" (often used in do-it-yourself kits and form books), which gives someone *total* freedom to legally sign your name with *no* plan or instructions to follow.

What Happens If You Have Minor Children

If you have minor children, you will need to set up a children's trust *within your living trust* to prevent the court from taking control of the inheritance. Here's why. At the deaths of both you and your spouse, your back-up trustee will distribute your property and dissolve your trust. If you have minor children, your trust needs to specify that their inheritance goes immediately from your trust into one for your children. The children's trust "inherits" *for* your minor children—they do not directly receive the inheritance in their own names. This is what keeps the court from taking control of the inheritance through a probate guardianship. As long as the inheritance stays in a trust—first in yours, then in one for your children—you will avoid probate.

Your trust is prepared from your decisions

You will name a *trustee* to manage your children's inheritance and a *guardian* to raise them according to your written instructions. The trustee and guardian can be the same person or different people. The court must still approve the guardian, but this is only a minor formality when compared to a probate guardianship in which the court also controls the inheritance. However, the court *cannot* overrule your choice of trustee, who will use the assets in the trust to care for your children until each reaches the age(s) you specify. And with your hand-picked trustee controlling the money, there may be no real incentive for an irresponsible "ex" to want custody of your children.

By having a children's trust within your living trust, there will be no courts, attorneys, cumbersome probate guardianships or delays involved with your children's inheritance, even if you become incapacitated. So your children's trustee and guardian will have much more flexibility, and will be able to respond more quickly, to meet your children's changing needs.

If you are a grandparent, you can set up a children's trust within your living trust to leave an inheritance to your grandchildren in the same way to prevent the possibility of a probate guardianship. We'll discuss this more in Part Four.

HOW A LIVING TRUST IS SET UP

An attorney prepares your living trust from *your* decisions about what you want to happen if you become disabled and when you die. *You* make the basic planning decisions—inventory your property, decide who you want to receive it when you die, name someone you trust to be responsible for its distribution, and someone to take care of you if you can no longer take care of yourself.

The attorney will make sure the living trust satisfies your state's legal requirements and will prepare it for you to sign. Trust documents are usually prepared from standardized trust forms (many commercial banks, trust companies and financial advisors have sample trust forms if you want to look at some basic trust provisions). Because living trusts are traditional and well-established in estate planning, your attorney will probably not need to create something completely new and customized for you. In fact, most people only need one basic trust document to handle all their needs and property. This may sound pretty simple and it is—*as long as* you use an estate planning attorney who is experienced in doing living trusts and can make the necessary modifications to handle *your* family's situation. It is very important that your living trust is done properly.

After your attorney has prepared your living trust document and you have read and approved it, you sign the trust and it is notarized. You then change the titles and account names for all of your titled property (real estate, checking and savings accounts, safe deposit boxes, investments, car, etc.) from your name to the name of your trust. You will also change beneficiary designations to your trust (we'll discuss this in just a moment).

Don't Leave Your Living Trust Unfunded

Your living trust is unfunded if you have signed your trust document but haven't changed the titles of your property to your trust. But you don't want to leave your living trust unfunded—anything you leave out of your trust will probably have to go through probate. *The only way to completely avoid probate is to put everything you own into your trust.*

You should be suspicious if someone tells you that you only need to place one asset (or maybe one dollar) into your living trust to fund it. This may be appropriate with some other kinds of trusts (a life insurance trust, for example, is not funded until the insured dies and the proceeds are paid to the trust—we'll explain more about life insurance trusts in Part Five.) But this is *not* what you want to do with your *living* trust. You are setting up a living trust to avoid probate—and the only way it can do that is if you place your assets into it.

Putting Property Into Your Trust

Changing the names on titles is not that hard to do. As an example, let's look at how you would put your home into your trust.

Let's say you and your spouse own your home jointly and the title says "John and Mary Smith, husband and wife." Let's also assume you signed your trust on January 1, 1990. To change the titles to your trust, you both just sign a "correction deed" (in some states, you use a quitclaim or trust transfer deed), changing the title from your individual names to "John and Mary Smith, Trustees under trust dated January 1, 1990" and record the deed. That's all there is to it. If you later decide to sell your house, you would sign the deed as "John and Mary Smith, Trustees under trust dated January 1, 1990."

Everything you put in your living trust will avoid probate

The reason you use a correction deed is that you are simply *correcting the title*—you are not *selling* the property. (Remember, a living trust is revocable—you can always change your mind about any property you put into it. This is very different from selling, which is an irrevocable action.) In most states, this will not trigger a re-assessment of your property taxes or disturb your current mortgage in any way. Your attorney can help you do this or do it for you. (In fact, many attorneys automatically will change the title of your home *for* you when they prepare your trust document.) Just make sure your attorney understands you want a *correction* of title, not a *transfer* of title.

Titled Property

Almost any kind of property can be held in your trust, including any out-of-state property you own. Typical trust property includes real estate (like your home) and other property with formal titles (such as checking and savings accounts, stocks, insurance, mutual funds, etc.).

Some of these—such as stocks, securities and notes payable to you—can be *assigned* to your trust without having to be retitled. Rather than taking actual possession of the original certificates and changing the names on each of them, we suggest that you have your banker or broker keep your stocks, bonds, etc. in a custodial account for you in the name of your trust. This is much faster and easier, and since most brokers and bankers are insured, you don't have to worry about misplacing certificates or losing them in a fire, etc.

In Part Four we have included a section on how to put different kinds of property into your trust. Don't worry about having to handle all of the paperwork yourself—usually a professional (your banker, attorney, investment broker, life insurance agent, etc.) can help you make sure everything is done properly.

Untitled Property

Of course, many types of property (such as jewelry, art, clothes, and home furnishings) do not have formal title documents. You do not have to inventory or list these to include them in your trust. The standard provisions of most living trust documents will automatically "sweep" all of your untitled property and personal belongings into your trust.

Change Beneficiary Designations

Beneficiary proceeds (for example, from insurance policies or credit union accounts) as a rule are not subject to probate. They are intended to be available immediately upon death, paid directly to the beneficiary *outside* of the probate process. However, to prevent the *possibility* of probate, you should change beneficiary designations to your living trust. Here's why.

If your beneficiary is incompetent when you die, the court will set up a conservatorship on his/her behalf and control the proceeds—even if you have a living trust. If, on the other hand, your *trust* is listed as beneficiary, the proceeds will be paid to your trust, and your back-up trustee will be able to use the funds to care for your beneficiary—without court involvement.

Here's another reason. Many beneficiary designation forms only provide space for you to name one beneficiary. But what if both you and your named beneficiary die at the same time? Unless you had named a secondary (or contingent) beneficiary, the court will have to decide who will receive the proceeds. You can avoid this by naming your trust as the beneficiary and including instructions in your trust for distribution of these proceeds.

In addition, having all of your assets (including these benefits) flow through your living trust is a very convenient way to coordinate your total estate plan through one document.

Possible Exception—Tax-Deferred Savings Plans

Even with these risks, there may be valid tax reasons to list your spouse instead of your living trust as primary beneficiary on tax-deferred savings plans, such as your IRA, retirement savings plan (like a 401(k)), pension plan, Keogh, etc. Here's why.

Because these are tax-deferred plans, you did not pay income taxes on this money when it was deposited. The income taxes are deferred until you withdraw the money at a later time—ideally, at your retirement when your income (and tax bracket) is lower. So, sooner or later, these income taxes will have to be paid.

If your spouse is the beneficiary, when you die he/she will have several options on how to receive this money. If, for example, the distribution is to be

You keep full control over everything in your living trust

received in a lump sum, your spouse can "roll over" the proceeds into his/her IRA, further delaying payment of taxes until age 70 1/2. But with this option, as we just explained, you risk probate if your spouse is disabled when you die—or if you both should die at the same time.

If, on the other hand, your trust is the beneficiary, you do not run the risk of these proceeds being probated. But the income taxes must be paid when the proceeds are paid to your trust (upon your death). However, proceeds paid from a "qualified" plan (such as a Keogh or company-sponsored retirement plan), may qualify for special tax treatment known as five-year or ten-year averaging, which can reduce your tax liability.

Many couples prefer that this money be available for the surviving spouse immediately upon the death of the first, and decide to make their trust the primary beneficiary—even though the income taxes will have to be paid at that time instead of later. If you do decide to name your spouse as primary beneficiary, you should name your trust as secondary beneficiary. Of course, this is something you and your spouse should discuss together and with your personal tax advisor.

What About Naming My Estate As Beneficiary?

For some reason, a surprising number of people name "my estate" as their beneficiary. As we just explained, beneficiary proceeds are intended to be available to the beneficiary immediately upon death *outside* of probate. But if you name your estate as the beneficiary, you're *guaranteeing* the proceeds will go through probate. Think about this for a moment—*who* is "my estate?" The probate court will have to decide—it will collect the funds and distribute them along with any other probated assets *after* the probate process is completed. Besides taking longer to reach your beneficiaries, a good portion of the proceeds will be lost to probate fees.

More About Your Life Insurance

In addition to making your trust the beneficiary, you should also change ownership of any insurance policies to your living trust. This way, if you become incompetent, your back-up trustee could borrow on the cash value of the policy if needed to help pay for your care. (However, if you are single and your net estate is more than $600,000, or if you are married and it is more than

$1.2 million, you should probably consider having an irrevocable life insurance trust in addition to your living trust to reduce estate taxes. We'll discuss this more in Part Five.)

THE ADVANTAGES OF A LIVING TRUST TO YOU AND YOUR FAMILY

Avoids Probate—Saves Money

By avoiding probate, you save thousands of dollars in probate costs. So now, instead of a big chunk of your hard-earned and carefully-managed assets and investments going to the probate system, it will *all* go to your beneficiaries.

You Keep Control

The trust document outlines your instructions for managing your assets and distributing them after your death or if you become incompetent. So even when you cannot handle your own affairs, you can make sure they are handled the way *you* want. Until that happens, you can sell trust property, change your beneficiaries, or even cancel the entire trust at any time, for any reason.

Takes Less Time

Distribution of your property when you die can usually be done in just a few weeks (a little longer for larger estates), instead of months or years. If you become physically or mentally incapacitated, your back-up trustee (or co-trustee) immediately takes control for you—there are no court delays or interferences.

Maintains Your Privacy

A living trust is private. If you become incompetent, it will remain a private family affair. When you die, no announcements have to be placed in the paper, no one is invited to contest it, and it is not part of the public court records. No information about your assets, beneficiaries or trustees will ever be made public. It is so private that disgruntled heirs or opportunity seekers who might have contested your will may not even know you have died.

A living trust *can* be contested, but not nearly as easily as a will. With a will, *anyone* can come forward and claim to have a right to part of your estate—without having to hire an attorney. And it's very easy to find out about your estate when notices of the probate proceedings appear in the papers.

But to contest a trust, the left out "heir" must hire a lawyer and file civil suit. Since the assets are not frozen under a living trust (as they are with a will), the trustee can go ahead and distribute them to the beneficiaries. The dissatisfied heir must then sue each beneficiary individually, which is expensive and time consuming. This complicated process will usually discourage even the greediest "heir" from contesting your wishes.

Minimizes Emotional Stress

With the court restrictions removed, your family can continue their normal day-to-day routines much more easily. All of your affairs can be handled quickly and easily. If you are incompetent, your family can look after your care in privacy. And when you die, they can grieve your passing privately and get on with their own lives without the frustration of prolonged court proceedings.

Inexpensive (And Easy) To Set Up

You will probably pay a little more to set up a living trust than you would to have a will prepared. But don't forget that the true cost of a will also includes the costs of probate. So, while a living trust may cost more initially, in the long run it will save your family money. Also, with living trusts becoming more popular, prices are getting competitive (some attorneys have flat rates or "package" prices). So you may not even have to pay much more to begin with.

How much you end up paying will depend on how complicated your plan is, the type and amount of your assets, if you need additional tax planning, etc. If you establish a trust with tax-saving provisions (as we'll discuss in Part Three), a portion of the attorney's fees may be tax deductible.

You can also help keep the cost of your living trust down. Remember, when you're talking with your attorney, you're "on the clock." You don't want to spend a lot of unnecessary time "chit-chatting" about living trusts and having him/her educate you about the general concept. Use your attorney's time and your money wisely—be specific with your questions as they relate to your individual situation. The more you know about living trusts and the more organized and prepared you are, the more you will save on attorney fees. Reading this book and completing the Personal and Financial Organizer will help you make your decisions, get organized and keep your costs down.

A living trust is private, saves time and money

You can complete your part of setting up your living trust in just a few hours. The attorney should have the first draft of the documents ready for you to review within a couple of weeks. You should probably allow another couple of weeks to review them and have any changes made. How long it will actually take will depend on how quickly you can respond, if you want any special provisions in your trust, and how busy your attorney is.

No Special Government Forms Are Required

As long as you are your own trustee or co-trustee, you do not need a separate tax identification number or need to file a separate tax return for your living trust. You continue to use your social security number and file the same personal income tax returns as before. When your back-up trustee takes over for you, or if you decide to name someone else as your trustee, he/she will need to apply for a tax identification number and file a separate tax return for the trust. A qualified CPA, tax attorney or corporate trustee can provide assistance if needed.

Low Maintenance—Easy To Change

Setting up your living trust is usually a one-time charge. And once it is set up, it requires very little maintenance. You will only need to see your attorney if you make changes to the actual document—if you change your trustee, a back-up trustee or beneficiary; decide to disinherit (or re-inherit) someone; etc. To make these kinds of changes to your document, your attorney can prepare an amendment for a nominal cost—you don't need to have your trust redone.

You also will not need to have your trust changed as you buy and sell property. To sell trust property, you sign the papers as trustee of your trust. As you acquire new property, you just title it in the name of your trust.

Special Gifts Are Easy—And Inexpensive—With A Living Trust

You will probably want to give certain items (of either real or sentimental value) to specific people and/or organizations. With a living trust, this is easy.

All you have to do is take a separate sheet of paper, make a list of these gifts (including titled property) and who you want to have them, have the list notarized, and keep it with your living trust document. If you change your mind, just make a new list and have it notarized. You don't have to go back

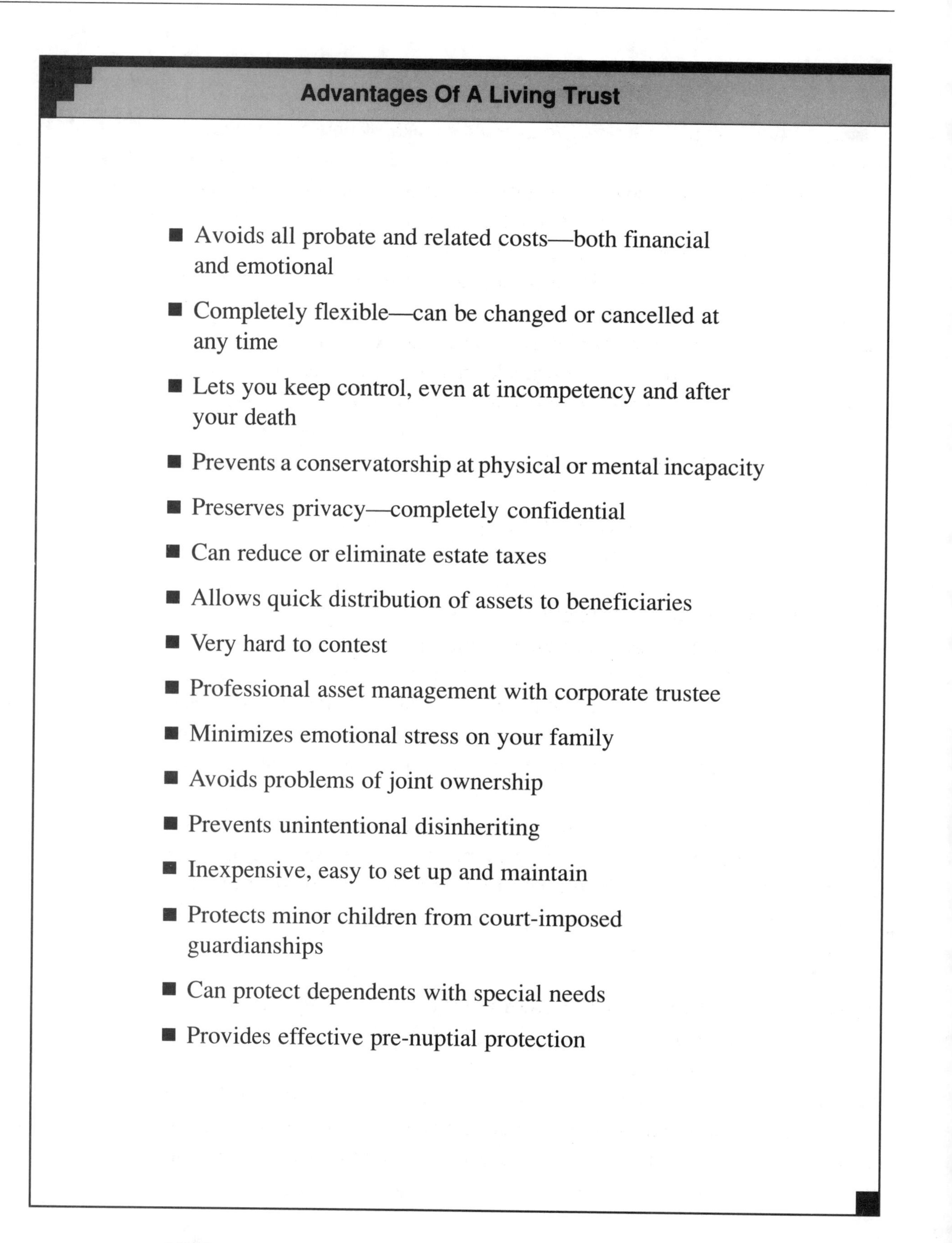

Advantages Of A Living Trust

- Avoids all probate and related costs—both financial and emotional
- Completely flexible—can be changed or cancelled at any time
- Lets you keep control, even at incompetency and after your death
- Prevents a conservatorship at physical or mental incapacity
- Preserves privacy—completely confidential
- Can reduce or eliminate estate taxes
- Allows quick distribution of assets to beneficiaries
- Very hard to contest
- Professional asset management with corporate trustee
- Minimizes emotional stress on your family
- Avoids problems of joint ownership
- Prevents unintentional disinheriting
- Inexpensive, easy to set up and maintain
- Protects minor children from court-imposed guardianships
- Can protect dependents with special needs
- Provides effective pre-nuptial protection

to your attorney and change your trust document—you can do it at home. Your new notarized list is a legally recognized amendment to your living trust. So you can make changes any time and as often as you like.

With a will, this would be a lot more complicated and expensive. Most states permit you to make a separate list of your Special Gifts, but it is usually limited to just your personal property (no cash or any titled property). To specify who you want to receive your *titled* property (such as real estate, investments, bank accounts, etc.) or cash, it has to be specifically listed in your will, which is prepared by an attorney, and witnessed. If you change your mind, you have to go back to your attorney, he/she will add an amendment (codicil) and have it witnessed. As you might expect, this can get expensive and take a lot of time.

Even though this is much easier with a living trust, you'll want to be careful with special gifts of substantial value (like real estate) or if your estate is sizeable—you may need some tax planning with your living trust. It's a good idea to have your attorney review your list to avoid possible tax problems.

Effective Pre-Nuptial Protection

A living trust also provides very effective pre-nuptial protection for your property. That's because any property you put into your living trust *before you marry* remains the property of that trust, and stays separate from property accumulated *during* your marriage—even in community property states. Just be careful not to combine assets acquired before and after the marriage.

It is not uncommon to have three living trusts in one family—each spouse has a separate living trust for property acquired *before* the marriage (usually giving it to his/her respective children from a previous marriage or to other relatives), and they have a joint living trust for property acquired *during* the marriage.

Reduce Or Eliminate Estate Taxes With Your Living Trust

Your living trust can also reduce or even eliminate estate taxes. A full explanation of how this is done is found in Part Three, which comes next. The same planning which reduces estate taxes also has other benefits—including providing for a surviving spouse and keeping control over who will receive certain assets. So even if you don't think you need the tax planning, you will want to read through this section.

ARE THERE ANY DISADVANTAGES OF A LIVING TRUST?

Not really. What some people view as a disadvantage usually turns out to be either bad information or, at the most, only a minor inconvenience—especially when you compare it to the many advantages a living trust can provide. Let's take a look at some you may have heard.

A Living Trust Is More Expensive Than A Will

It usually does cost more to set up a living trust than it does to do a will. But the cost of a will really includes the costs of probate. A living trust, on the other hand, avoids all probate—so, when you realistically compare the two, a living trust is quite a bargain.

It Takes Time To Change Titles And Beneficiary Designations

Yes, it does take some time to change all of the titles and beneficiary designations to your living trust. Of course, how much time it takes for *you* will depend on how many different assets you own that have titles and beneficiary designations. But, for most people, this is only a one-time event. As you buy and sell property, it shouldn't take any more time for you to sign your name as the trustee of your trust than it does to sign your name as an individual.

Instead of putting this off, it's best to just make this process a priority and don't stop until everything has been changed to your trust. If you "drag this out" and transfer property when you get around to it, it could take you a long time to get this job completed—or worse, you may never get around to finishing it.

Refinancing Property Is Inconvenient

If the people at your bank or savings and loan are unfamiliar with living trusts, they may be reluctant to refinance property that is titled in the name of your trust. This is primarily because mortgages are often re-sold to institutions in the secondary lending market, and they won't buy mortgages in the name of a trust because they are afraid some trusts may have special restrictions preventing a trustee from mortgaging or selling the property. With living trusts becoming more common, this doesn't happen as often as it used to. But if you find this becoming a problem for you, it may be easier to transfer the title back to your name *temporarily* (just until the loan has been approved and closed). Then *make sure* you transfer the property back into your trust as soon as possible.

Compared to the costs of a will, a living trust is quite a bargain

Problems With ATM Withdrawals

If you use a credit card to withdraw cash from your personal checking account through an ATM (automatic teller machine), you may run into a problem. Most banks will not issue a credit card in the name of a trust, and for the ATM to work, the names on the account and the credit card must match. So if your personal checking account is in the name of your trust and your credit card is in your name, the ATM won't work. If this turns out to be a problem for you, you can make the withdrawal as a cash advance against the credit card itself, instead of against your checking account.

If your bank issues a separate ATM withdrawal card, you'll probably be okay. However, some banks may still be hesitant to issue one to a trust account if they're not sure who is authorized to use it. So they may ask to see your trust document before approving it (if so, a Certificate of Trust, as explained in Part Four, may satisfy this requirement). Of course, if you have a good relationship with your bank, you probably won't have a problem.

Loss Of Bankruptcy Protection

In some states, a portion or all of your home is automatically protected from creditors if you file for bankruptcy. When you place your home in your living trust, you may lose this protection. But the *amount* of protection you forfeit will depend on the state in which you live—and it may be so insignificant that it doesn't matter. For example, in Missouri only the first $12,500 of a personal residence can be protected from bankruptcy—certainly not enough to warrant leaving your home (the most valuable asset most people own) out of your living trust. If you are considering filing for bankruptcy, you may want to ask your attorney about the bankruptcy laws in your state.

There's No Time Limit On Creditors' Claims

It is true that opening a probate after your death limits the length of time creditors have to present claims (including lawsuits) against your estate. No claims are usually permitted after this time period has passed.

In most states, a living trust does not provide for this. Although the normal statute of limitations would still apply, a lawsuit could be filed against your beneficiaries after the assets have been distributed (although this is a costly and tedious procedure, as we explained on page 64). Because of this, you may have heard that those professionals who are at a greater risk of being sued than others (for example, doctors and attorneys) should have wills instead of living trusts.

However, even if you are at risk for being sued, you can and should have a living trust—and you can still benefit from the time limit on claims that probate provides. To do this, you set up your living trust just as we have explained, and transfer all of your property into it. Then, when you die, your co-trustee or back-up trustee can open a probate to see if any creditors have claims to present. If they do, then *just enough assets to satisfy the claim(s)* can be transferred out of your living trust—the rest are protected from probate. So, even if you are at high risk for claims against your estate, you can limit the time on these claims *and* get the protection that a living trust provides.

However, as living trusts have become more popular, laws have recently been passed in some states so that a living trust can now also have a limit on the length of time creditors have to present claims to the trustee (similar legislation is also pending in other states). So, in these states, even if you are in one of these high risk professions, you can accomplish the same thing through your living trust—with *no* probate.

Summary

For most people, the things we just mentioned either never come up or don't present a problem—any inconvenience is more than offset by the many advantages a living trust can provide.

Usually the only problem people have with properly prepared living trusts has nothing to do with the trust itself, but with property that was left out of the trust because they failed to change all of the titles and appropriate beneficiary designations. Sometimes people forget something, but usually they just procrastinate. The trust still works—but any property left out of it risks being probated. And probate is exactly what you don't want.

WHY AREN'T LIVING TRUSTS BETTER KNOWN?

If living trusts are such a wonderful thing, why don't we hear as much about them as we do about wills?

One reason is, because the legal profession has become so specialized, a lot of attorneys don't know about living trusts. Unless they specialize in estate planning, they probably weren't even exposed to living trusts in law school. But wills, on the other hand, are so common that most attorneys feel they can do them. So it's easier for them to draw up standard wills than take the extra time to learn about something that isn't their specialty. It also takes time to educate a client. So they usually stick with what they (and their clients) know.

Another is that the legal profession has become very competitive and some attorneys don't want to risk losing clients. Rather than refer a client to another attorney who specializes in living trusts, they may not bring up the subject. So, unless you specifically ask about a living trust, your attorney may not take the initiative to tell you about something he/she doesn't do.

Then, as in all professions, there are those who don't think of your best interests first. These attorneys earn a substantial part of their living from the probate system, and are more than happy to draft your will for a nominal charge while you are living—because they stand an excellent chance of probating your will when you die. In fact, some may encourage you to name them as the attorney to represent your estate in probate.

This is called "building a will file"—they wait for you to die so they can collect legal fees from your estate when it goes through probate. And, if you become incompetent or leave minor children, they will probably represent you or your children in a conservatorship or guardianship case, which can also be a very lucrative source of attorney fees. Remember, one of the biggest expenses of probate is attorney fees, which can easily run into many thousands of dollars. Not too many of these attorneys are eager to do living trusts because they avoid probate, cutting off a substantial source of future income.

For these and other reasons, most people haven't heard of living trusts. So they usually ask for wills when they go to see attorneys about estate planning. And if you ask an attorney for a will or for the least expensive way to plan your estate, then you'll probably get a will. But if you ask for the best way to plan your estate, the attorney might recommend a living trust—but then again, as we've just explained, he or she might not.

In any event, *don't* give up or try to do this yourself. You *need* a competent estate planning attorney, and there are many excellent ones who are very familiar with living trusts, believe in them and do them on a regular basis. In fact, today, more and more people are finding out about living trusts, and in response to the public's growing awareness and demand for them, there are some attorneys and law firms who now specialize in living trusts.

These attorneys feel a moral and ethical responsibility to educate their clients about living trusts as an alternative to probate. This is the kind of attorney you want to advise you and help you set up yours. In Part Four we'll give you information to help you find one of these attorneys.

A Comparison At A Glance

	With No Will	With A Will	With A Living Trust
At Disability	*Probate:* Court appoints conservator/guardian who oversees your care, must keep detailed records and reports to the court. Court controls all your finances and assets, approves all expenses.	*Probate:* Same as with no will.	*No probate:* Your back-up trustee manages your financial affairs according to your instructions for as long as necessary. (In some states, conservator/guardian may be required for health care decisions.)
Court Costs	You pay all court costs, legal fees.	Same as with no will.	None.
At Death	*Probate:* Court orders your debts paid and possessions distributed according to state law, which may not be what you would have wanted.	*Probate:* After verifying your will, court orders your debts paid and possessions distributed according to your will.	*No probate:* Debts are paid and possessions immediately distributed to beneficiaries by back-up trustee according to your written instructions.
Court Costs	Your estate pays all court costs and legal fees (often estimated at 5-10% of the gross value of your estate, higher if your will is contested.)	Same as with no will.	None.
Time	Usually 1-2 years or more before heirs can inherit.	Same as with no will.	Usually 4-6 weeks for smaller estates; a little longer for larger ones.
Flexibility and Control	*None*: Your property is controlled and distributed by probate court according to state law. Very easy for anyone to contest.	*Limited*: You can change your will any time, but it can easily be contested. Family has no control over probate costs or delays.	*Total*: You can change your trust at any time, even discontinue it. Your property remains under total control of your trust, even if you are disabled. Hard to contest.
Privacy	*None*: Probate proceedings are public record. Exposes family to unscrupulous solicitors and greedy heirs.	*None*: Same as with no will.	*Total*: Privacy preserved. No probate. Living trusts are not public record.
Minor Child	Probate court controls inheritance, appoints guardian. All decisions and financial transactions require court approval. Child receives full inheritance at legal age.	Same as with no will. Children's trust in will provides limited protection, but will must be probated first and cannot go into effect at your physical or mental incapacity.	No probate. Your appointed trustee manages inheritance and provides funds for expenses until child reaches age(s) you specify. Court approves guardian, but cannot overrule your choice of trustee and has no control over inheritance.
Cost	All court costs and attorney fees are paid from child's inheritance.	Same as with no will.	None.

Part Three

HOW TO REDUCE/ ELIMINATE ESTATE TAXES AND MORE

(The ABCs Of A Living Trust)

Part Three—

HOW TO REDUCE/ELIMINATE ESTATE TAXES AND MORE (THE ABCs OF A LIVING TRUST)

You know by now that if you use a living trust, you avoid probate and all expenses connected with it. But so far we haven't talked about the *taxes* that must be paid at death. You may be surprised to learn that your living trust can also reduce or eliminate these as well.

In this section, we'll explain how additional provisions can be included in your living trust that provide valuable tax planning and other benefits—such as how you can provide for your surviving spouse yet keep control of certain assets, and how you can protect assets in the event you or your spouse suffer a catastrophic illness or injury. So, even if you don't have to worry about estate taxes, these provisions can provide valuable protection.

INCOME TAXES vs. ESTATE TAXES

Now, to avoid any confusion, let's first explain the two kinds of taxes that must be paid when you die—*income taxes* and *estate taxes.*

Income Taxes

Regardless of whether or not you have a living trust, your estate must file a final federal income tax return, just as you do every year. (Depending on the state in which you live, you may also pay state income taxes.) Any income you receive in the year you die must be reported and any taxes due on that income must be paid. *Your living trust has no effect whatsoever on income taxes.* However, your accountant may be able to provide some assistance in lowering your taxable income.

Federal estate taxes start at 37%

Estate Taxes

The other tax is the federal estate tax (also called a death tax). If the *net* value of your estate (the value of all of your assets minus your debts) is more than $600,000 when you die, federal estate taxes must be paid from your estate before it is distributed to your beneficiaries—beginning at a tax rate of 37%. This is, in effect, a "double" tax. Over the years, you've already paid income taxes on the money and assets that now make up your estate. And unless you plan ahead, your estate may have to pay taxes on these assets *again*. But with proper planning, your living trust *can* reduce or eliminate these estate taxes.

Determining Your Net Estate

If you think your estate isn't large enough to be affected by estate taxes, you *could* just skip over this section. But before you do, think for a moment. If you own a home or other real estate, it could be worth a lot more than you think—real estate can easily appreciate in value over the years (especially in certain parts of the country) and can continue to appreciate after you or your spouse die.

To determine the current size of your net estate, you add up the current market value of everything you own and subtract any debts and mortgages. (The *Personal and Financial Organizer* in the back of this book will help you do this easily.)

Assets include real estate, automobiles, boats, campers, checking and savings accounts, investments (including CDs, stocks, bonds and mutual funds), profit sharing balances, IRAs, pensions, investments in partnerships and/or businesses, notes payable to you, any personal property you own, and any other benefits to which your estate will be entitled when you die.

Your assets also include (this one may surprise you) the death benefits from *all* life insurance policies on your life for which you have any *incidents of ownership* as defined by the IRS. This would include policies for which you pay premiums, have the right to name (and change) the beneficiary, borrow against the policy, assign it, etc.—regardless of who actually *owns* the policy. For example, insurance provided by your employer would be included if you can name and/or change the beneficiary. (A more complete discussion of this is found in Part Five.)

Don't forget that many assets will appreciate between now and when you die, and estate taxes are based on the fair market value as of the date of your death. Use a little quick arithmetic and $600,000 may not be so far away.

The Marital Deduction—Uncle Sam's Plan

Now, what do you do about these estate taxes? You may not know it, but you already have a plan to reduce estate taxes when you die if you are married. You didn't sit down and plan it—Uncle Sam did it for you. It's called the *marital deduction* and this is how it works. When you die, you can leave any amount of assets (real estate, personal property, investments, etc.) to your spouse and it will not be taxed at your death. There is no limit on the value of assets one spouse can leave to the other tax-free.

So, that sounds pretty good—so far. But when your surviving spouse dies, the *full* amount of the estate (what your spouse owns plus what you left your spouse) will be taxed before it can go to any of your beneficiaries. And, depending on how much longer your spouse lives, it could be worth substantially more than when you died. The estate *is* entitled to claim a tax exemption. Currently the amount is equal to $600,000, so the first $600,000 of the estate can go to your heirs tax-free.

But guess what? *Both* you and your spouse were entitled to a $600,000 exemption—*if you had planned ahead.* But you didn't use yours and wasted your $600,000 exemption. You and your spouse *could* have passed on up to $1.2 million to your beneficiaries tax-free, but now the estate is only entitled to *one* $600,000 exemption (your surviving spouse's exemption). Uncle Sam is very patient (and smart)—he'll wait until your surviving spouse dies and gamble that he'll collect more taxes on a much larger estate!

(*Note*: If you look at a federal estate tax return, you will see that, after a few calculations, the actual tax on the first $600,000 of an estate is $192,800—but you get a *tax credit* of $192,800. So there are no estate taxes due on the first $600,000 of an estate—it is *exempt* from estate taxes. For ease of explanation, we refer to this as a $600,000 *exemption.*)

Some people don't think their estates are worth anything close to $600,000 so they don't worry about tax planning. But keep this in mind—people are living longer (particularly women, who often outlive their husbands by many years) and even a small estate can increase tremendously in value over time, especially if you own a home or other real estate, or if you have substantial life insurance.

Of course, the choice is yours. You can do nothing and use Uncle Sam's plan. Or you can plan ahead—your living trust can be set up to avoid probate *and* reduce or even eliminate estate taxes. Here's how.

THE A-B LIVING TRUST SOLUTION

You and your spouse can set up one common living trust (just like we've been discussing), of which each of you owns half. When one of you dies, this trust will automatically split into two *separate* trusts. This is called an "A-B living trust" because the two separate trusts are typically referred to as Trust A (for the surviving spouse) and Trust B (for the deceased).

To help keep these straight, think of Trust A as the one "**A**bove the ground" (for the living person) and Trust B as "**B**elow the ground" (for the deceased). It is a bit "direct" but, as a word association trick, it works.

If the value of the common trust is no more than $1.2 million, half of the value of the assets are placed in Trust A and half in Trust B. Each trust will be entitled to a $600,000 exemption—Trust B uses the deceased's exemption and Trust A will use the surviving spouse's exemption later when he/she dies and the assets in both trusts are distributed to the beneficiaries. So, assuming Trust A does not grow to more than $600,000 by that time, the entire estate will be exempt from estate taxes.

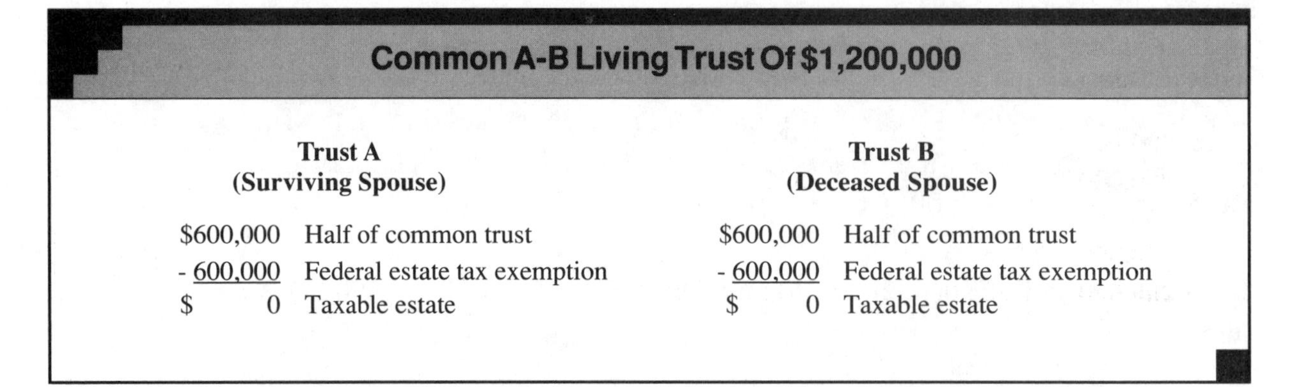

Common A-B Living Trust Of $1,200,000

Trust A (Surviving Spouse)		**Trust B (Deceased Spouse)**	
$600,000	Half of common trust	$600,000	Half of common trust
- 600,000	Federal estate tax exemption	- 600,000	Federal estate tax exemption
$ 0	Taxable estate	$ 0	Taxable estate

If the trust is more than $1.2 million, usually only $600,000 of the deceased's half is placed in Trust B, since this is the amount of the estate tax exemption. The rest is added to Trust A (the surviving spouse's trust). There are no estate taxes on Trust B because it doesn't exceed the $600,000 exemption. And there are none due now on the rest of the deceased's estate because it is transferred toTrust A using the marital deduction. Later, when the surviving spouse dies, his/her exemption is used—so another $600,000 is exempt from estate taxes.

Common A-B Living Trust Of $1,500,000

Trust A (Surviving Spouse)		Trust B (Deceased Spouse)	
$750,000	Half of common trust	$750,000	Half of common trust
+ 150,000	Excess from deceased's estate via marital deduction	- 150,000	Excess transferred to Trust A via marital deduction
$900,000	Balance	$600,000	Balance
- 600,000	Federal estate tax exemption	- 600,000	Federal estate tax exemption
$300,000	Taxable estate	$ 0	Taxable estate

By using an A-B living trust, you and your spouse can leave up to $1.2 million *estate tax-free* to your beneficiaries—*and with no probate costs.* If you use a simple will (as many couples do) or have no estate plan, and rely on just the marital deduction for your tax planning, you would only be able to use *one* $600,000 exemption—and, under current law, *approximately $235,000* in federal estate taxes would have to be paid on the $1.2 million estate, plus thousands of dollars in probate fees.

	With A Simple Will			With An A-B Living Trust		
Estate Size	*Estate Taxes*	*Probate Fees**	*Total*	*Estate Taxes*	*Probate Fees*	*Total*
$ 100,000	$ 0	$ 6,300	$ 6,300	$ 0	$ 0	$ 0
300,000	0	14,300	14,300	0	0	0
600,000	0	26,300	26,300	0	0	0
750,000	55,500	32,300	87,800	0	0	0
1,200,000	235,000	46,300	281,300	0	0	0

**California's probate fees, which are about average for most states.*

Leave up to $1.2 million to your children estate tax-free, with no probate

This is not a tax shelter or some tricky way to avoid paying taxes. The estate *is* being taxed when both spouses die—you are both simply using the exemptions to which you are entitled.

In addition to saving estate taxes with your A-B living trust, you can provide for your surviving spouse, even after the assets have been divided into two separate trusts. Let's assume, for ease of explanation, that the husband dies first. When the assets are divided into Trust A and Trust B, his wife now has complete control over Trust A and can do whatever she wants with its assets (remember, this is now her trust). In addition, she can receive any income generated by Trust B for as long as she lives and can even withdraw from the principal if needed for health, education, maintenance and support.

There are some restrictions if she receives money from Trust B for other reasons, but these areas cover anything she would need for normal living expenses. She cannot have 100% control over the assets in Trust B, because that would legally give her ownership of them, causing them to be taxed when she dies. (Because of this, if you want your surviving spouse to be trustee of Trust B, your attorney may want a co-trustee named to act with your spouse.)

The surviving spouse, then, has complete control over her own trust (Trust A) plus, for the rest of her life, she can receive all the income from Trust B and principal from it when needed. And when she dies, the assets in both trusts (up to $600,000 each, a total of $1.2 million) will go to the beneficiaries estate tax-free—and without probate. Now, what could be better than that?

Dividing Assets Between Trust A And Trust B

If the total estate is over $1.2 million, the trustee will need to decide which of the deceased's assets will be placed in Trust B and which ones will transfer to Trust A through the marital deduction.

How do you know which assets to place into which trust? It would be smart to place into Trust B assets that will appreciate the most in value over the next few years. That's because the assets in Trust B are only valued and taxed when the first spouse dies. They are *not* re-valued later when the second spouse dies—and may be worth much more.

For example, let's say you have some investments that are worth $600,000 when you die and these are placed in Trust B. Again, no estate taxes will be

due at this time because the value of Trust B does not exceed your $600,000 exemption. Now, let's say that by the time your spouse dies, these assets have appreciated in value to over $1,000,000. *The full $1,000,000* will go to your beneficiaries *estate tax free* because the value of Trust B was "locked in" for estate tax purposes at the time of your death.

The assets that are placed in Trust A (the surviving spouse's trust) will not be valued and taxed until his/her death, which could be many years later. So it would be smart, if possible, to place into Trust A those assets that will appreciate more slowly.

Sometimes the division of assets is done on paper through bookkeeping, although some attorneys prefer to actually change titles from the *old* common trust to the *new* individual trusts (Trust A and Trust B). Of course, you don't have to worry about dividing the assets by yourself. It's a good idea to have a professional tax advisor or attorney involved to make sure everything is done properly and that your best tax planning options are utilized.

One Common Trust vs. Separate Trusts

You and your spouse could do the same thing we've been explaining with *separate* living trusts and have separate estates while you are both alive.

But most married couples who have built their estates together over the years are used to owning their property together, and usually prefer having one common living trust. It's much simpler because there is only one document to deal with and the assets do not have to be divided until one spouse dies. If you also have some separately owned assets, they can usually be handled in the one common trust document.

However, it's not unusual to have *three* living trusts in one family—separate ones for property acquired *before* the marriage (or for inheritances), and a common trust for jointly owned property or property acquired *during* the marriage. An experienced estate planning attorney will be able to advise you on your best options.

By the way, you may run into an attorney who says you can't have a common A-B living trust and use both exemptions, but they are done all the time by many experienced estate planning attorneys. If your attorney says you can't do this, you may want to get a second opinion. You may also want to refer to page 181 for more on this.

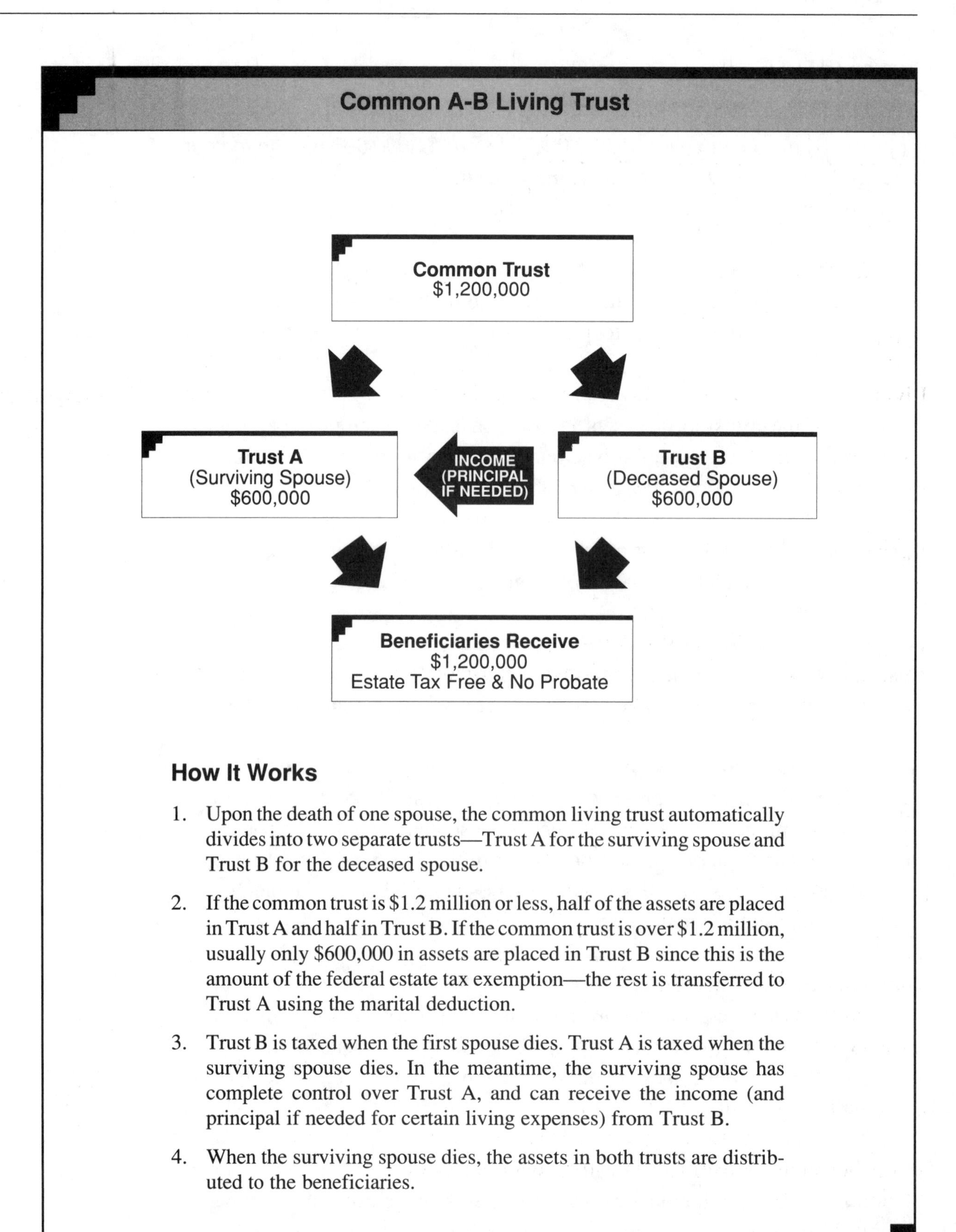

How It Works

1. Upon the death of one spouse, the common living trust automatically divides into two separate trusts—Trust A for the surviving spouse and Trust B for the deceased spouse.
2. If the common trust is $1.2 million or less, half of the assets are placed in Trust A and half in Trust B. If the common trust is over $1.2 million, usually only $600,000 in assets are placed in Trust B since this is the amount of the federal estate tax exemption—the rest is transferred to Trust A using the marital deduction.
3. Trust B is taxed when the first spouse dies. Trust A is taxed when the surviving spouse dies. In the meantime, the surviving spouse has complete control over Trust A, and can receive the income (and principal if needed for certain living expenses) from Trust B.
4. When the surviving spouse dies, the assets in both trusts are distributed to the beneficiaries.

Common A-B Living Trust

Advantages

- **Reduce/Eliminate Estate Taxes**—With an A-B living trust, you and your spouse can each use your $600,000 federal estate tax exemption. This lets you pass on to your beneficiaries up to $1.2 million estate tax-free and with no probate—saving approximately $235,000 in federal estate taxes, plus probate fees.
- **Provide For Surviving Spouse**—The surviving spouse has complete control over Trust A. In addition, he/she can receive the income (and principal, if needed for certain living expenses) from Trust B.
- **Control For First To Die**—After the first spouse dies and the common trust has been divided into Trust A and Trust B, no changes can be made to the provisions of Trust B—giving the first spouse to die complete control over who will eventually receive the assets in Trust B.
- **Estate Tax-Free Appreciation Of Trust B**—The assets placed in Trust B are valued and taxed only when the first spouse dies. There will be no re-valuation or estate taxes paid on any appreciation of these assets later when the surviving spouse dies and the assets in Trust B are distributed to the beneficiaries.
- **Protection Of Assets If Catastrophic Illness Strikes**—In the event of catastrophic illness or injury of the surviving spouse, the trust can be written to protect the assets in Trust B—so only the assets in Trust A will need to be "spent down" to qualify for valuable government assistance.

Other Advantages Of An A-B Living Trust

Additional Control

As we mentioned earlier in Part 2, one of the advantages of a common living trust is that either spouse automatically has control when the other becomes incompetent or dies. But unless an A-B provision is included in the trust, this also means the surviving spouse, as co-grantor, could later change something in the actual trust document—for example, the beneficiaries.

Now this may not be a concern for you. But let's say you have children from this or a previous marriage and you want to make sure they inherit your share of the trust property. What if your spouse later remarries? It is possible, even with a living trust, that the new husband or wife could end up inheriting everything (including your share) and your children could be disinherited—because your surviving spouse would be able to change the trust document.

But with the A-B provision in your living trust, this wouldn't happen because as soon as the first spouse dies and the common trust divides, Trust B (the deceased's trust) *cannot* be changed by anyone, not even by your surviving spouse. So you don't have to worry—if you name your children (or anyone else) as your beneficiaries, no one (not even your surviving spouse) will be able to change your instructions.

You do have the option, however, of giving your spouse limited ability to change beneficiaries of Trust B—if, for whatever reason, you want to do that. But, unless this provision is specifically included, your surviving spouse will *only* be able to make changes to Trust A (his/her trust).

Even if the assets in Trust B will eventually go to someone else, your spouse can continue to enjoy them. For example, if this is your second marriage and you die first, your spouse can continue to live in your home for the rest of his/her life. Then, when your spouse dies and the house is sold, your share of the proceeds will go to whomever you have named as beneficiary—your children from your first marriage, other relatives, etc.

Of course, there is no way for you to know now if your trust will be Trust A or Trust B (because you don't know which of you will die first). You simply specify that if you die first, certain instructions will apply to Trust B—such

Provide for your spouse and keep control

as who the beneficiaries are (like your children, a foundation, etc.) and any others you may wish to include. Your spouse, of course, will do the same.

Even if you don't need an A-B living trust for tax planning, you may want to consider one to make sure you keep control over who will receive your half of the estate.

Protection In The Event Of Catastrophic Illness

Here is another important reason to consider an A-B living trust if you have a modest estate and don't need the tax planning. If you or your spouse were to suffer a major illness or injury (perhaps a terminal condition), the medical expenses, even with insurance, would be substantial. To qualify for valuable government benefits, it is often necessary to "spend-down" the assets in the estate.

However, an A-B living trust can protect part of the estate after one spouse has died. The trust document can give the trustee *discretion* over whether or not to distribute income and principal from Trust B to the surviving spouse. Then, if the surviving spouse becomes seriously ill or injured and needs to qualify for government assistance, the trustee can decide not to provide any income or principal to the spouse. This prevents the assets in Trust B from being considered available to pay the surviving spouse's expenses. So only Trust A (the surviving spouse's trust) would have to be "spent down" in order to qualify for benefits—Trust B would be preserved for the beneficiaries.

Unfortunately, this doesn't help if one spouse becomes ill while you are both living. A certain amount of assets is usually exempted for the well spouse, but anything over that, including separately owned property, is usually considered available to pay the ill spouse's expenses. Of course, if you have a sizeable estate, it probably wouldn't make sense to spend down the assets just to qualify for government benefits—you'd pay for the medical expenses yourself. But this can be very valuable protection if you have a modest estate and need government assistance.

If Your Spouse Is Incompetent

To make sure you and your spouse will be able to use the two $600,000 exemptions to which you are entitled, your A-B living trust must be set up while both of you are alive and healthy. But if your spouse is already incompetent, you may still have some options.

Protect your assets if your spouse suffers a catastrophic illness

In some states, you can place your spouse in a conservatorship and request permission from the court to sign estate planning documents for your spouse (the *doctrine of substituted judgment* can sometimes be used for this purpose). This would allow you to do estate planning for your spouse, including setting up a living trust for him/her (or setting up a common A-B living trust for both of you).

You can then transfer your spouse's assets (his/her share of any jointly owned property and any separately owned assets) *out* of the conservatorship and *into* the trust, and request that the conservatorship file be closed. Very often the judge will agree in order to reduce the court's workload and if he/she believes the trustee will do a good job. (Having a corporate trustee involved, especially one the judge knows and has confidence in, will often help.)

Of course, you run the risk of the court not closing the file and staying involved—that decision will vary from judge to judge and from state to state. And you may run into some other problems. For example, if your spouse already has a will, you would have to convince the court that if your spouse were competent today, he/she would now want the trust instead of the will.

You will, of course, want to first check with your attorney to see if this is possible in your state. If your state doesn't allow this, *you should still set up your own living trust* to avoid probate of your share of the estate.

In fact, depending on the size of your estate, it may even be worthwhile to include an A-B provision so you would be able to use both $600,000 exemptions even if your spouse is incompetent. But this will only work if you die first. Here's why.

If you die first, Trust B (your trust) would use your $600,000 exemption and the remaining assets would go to your spouse's trust using the marital deduction. So no estate taxes would be paid at your death. The second $600,000 exemption would be used later when your spouse dies—just as we explained earlier.

But if your spouse dies first (which may happen, since your spouse is already ill) and doesn't have a trust, you would only be able to use one exemption (yours). To avoid paying estate taxes when your spouse dies, you would use the marital deduction to transfer your spouse's share of the assets to you. But when you die later, only one exemption (yours) can be used. Your spouse's exemption has been wasted—so only $600,000 will be exempt from estate taxes instead of $1.2 million.

Even if your state will not allow you to do estate planning for an incompetent spouse, you should have your own living trust so you can avoid probate on your half of the estate. And, if you do die first, you would be able to use both $600,000 exemptions.

These options should *not* take the place of planning your estate while you and your spouse are both healthy. But if your spouse is already incompetent, they may be worth investigating.

If Your Spouse Is Not A U.S. Citizen

If your spouse is not a citizen of the United States, he/she is no longer entitled to the marital deduction. This means that, without proper planning, anything in your estate over $600,000 will be taxed. To avoid this problem, your attorney will use a "qualified domestic trust" as part of your A-B living trust plan. If your spouse is not a U.S. citizen, make sure you tell your attorney at your first meeting—before your trust document is prepared.

THE A-B...AND NOW C

If you are married and your combined net estate is more than $1.2 million, you should know about the "A-B-C" living trust.

The "C" part is also called a "Q-TIP" trust, which stands for "qualified terminable interest property." It sounds complicated, but it really isn't. The fact that the surviving spouse must receive the income from Trust C and may have access to the principal under certain conditions is his/her "qualified interest" in the property. It is "terminable" because this "interest" ends when the surviving spouse dies.

The A-B-C Delays Additional Estate Taxes

This is not a way to avoid paying estate taxes if your estate is more than $1.2 million. You are already using your two estate tax exemptions through the A-B part of your living trust, so the portion of the estate placed in Trust C is not exempt from estate taxes. However, *payment* of estate taxes on this part of the estate will be *delayed* until the second death.

The advantage is that this leaves the estate intact. Since the estate has not been reduced by any estate taxes, a larger amount is available to invest and provide income to your surviving spouse. In addition, you are keeping more money available in case your spouse needs it. And, if your spouse does need part of the principal from Trust C, the estate may be worth less by the time your spouse dies—so you could end up paying *less* in estate taxes.

The A-B-C Provides Additional Control

An A-B-C living trust will also let you keep control over who will receive more of the estate than an A-B living trust would. Here's why.

If you use an A-B living trust and you die first, you will probably end up controlling who will receive only $600,000 of the estate. Since that's the amount of the estate tax exemption, usually that's all that is placed in Trust B—the rest usually goes to the surviving spouse's trust through the marital deduction to avoid paying any estate taxes at that time. So if, for example, your total estate is worth $1.5 million and you die first, you could end up controlling only $600,000 of the estate and your surviving spouse would control $900,000.

Common A-B Living Trust Of $1,500,000

Trust A (Surviving Spouse)		Trust B (Deceased Spouse)	
$750,000	Half of common trust	$750,000	Half of common trust
+ 150,000	Excess from deceased's estate via marital deduction	- 150,000	Excess transferred to Trust A via marital deduction
$900,000	Balance	$600,000	Balance

Of course, more than $600,000 can be placed in Trust B—giving you control over who will receive the proceeds—but estate taxes would have to be paid on the excess at the time of your death.

Now if you use an A-B-C living trust, you can make sure you each keep control of *half* of the estate—even if you die first. Let's again say your total estate is worth $1.5 million, and you die first. Upon your death, the estate will be split equally so that $750,000 goes into Trust A and $750,000 goes into Trust B. Trust B is further divided so that only $600,000 stays in Trust B (to take advantage of the $600,000 exemption) and the rest ($150,000) goes into Trust C, which will be taxed later when your surviving spouse dies and the assets in all three trusts are distributed to the beneficiaries.

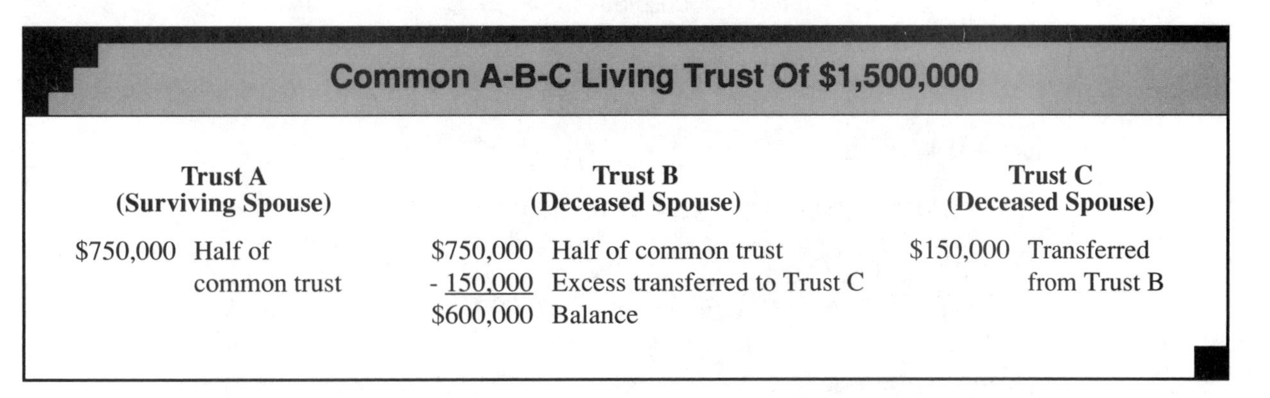

Common A-B-C Living Trust Of $1,500,000

Trust A (Surviving Spouse)		Trust B (Deceased Spouse)		Trust C (Deceased Spouse)	
$750,000	Half of common trust	$750,000	Half of common trust	$150,000	Transferred from Trust B
		- 150,000	Excess transferred to Trust C		
		$600,000	Balance		

Just as we explained earlier with the A-B trust, your surviving spouse has complete control over Trust A, can receive income from Trust B, and can also receive principal from Trust B, if needed, for health, education, maintenance and support. In addition, your spouse will receive all the income from Trust C and can also receive its principal, if needed, for these living expenses. When your spouse dies, the assets in both Trust B and Trust C (50% of the estate at the time of your death) will be distributed to the beneficiaries *you* specify.

Common A-B-C Living Trust

(For Estates Over $1.2 Million)

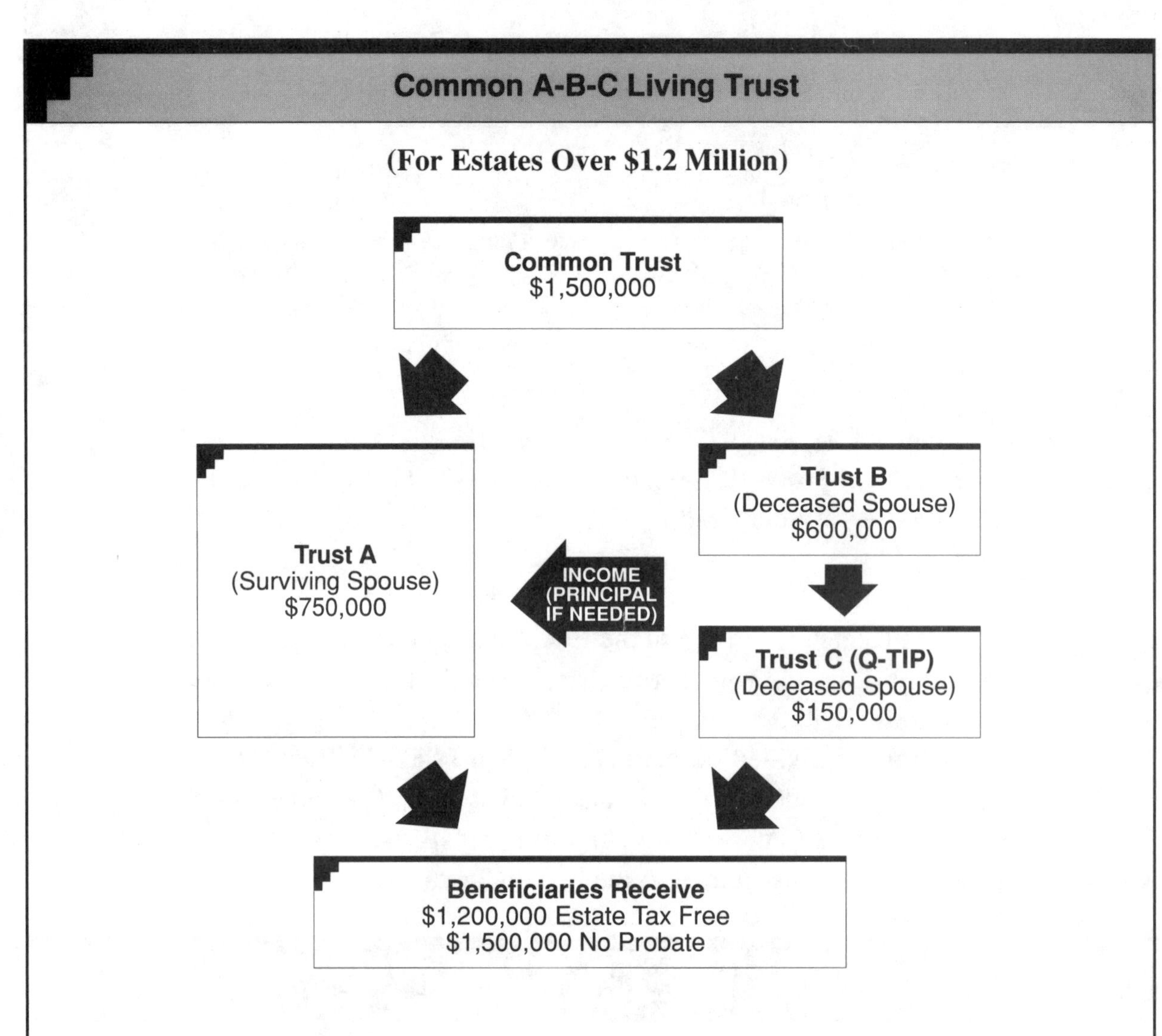

How It Works

1. Upon the death of one spouse, the common living trust is divided equally. Half of the estate goes into Trust A for the surviving spouse. The other half (the deceased spouse's share) is divided between Trust B and Trust C. Usually only $600,000 in assets are placed in Trust B since this is the amount of the federal estate tax exemption; the excess is placed into Trust C.

   As an example, in the illustration above, the total estate of $1.5 million is divided so that $750,000 (half) is placed in Trust A, and the other half is divided between Trust B ($600,000) and Trust C ($150,000).

Common A-B-C Living Trust

2. Trust B is taxed when the first spouse dies. Trust A and Trust C are taxed when the surviving spouse dies. In the meantime, the surviving spouse has complete control over Trust A, and can receive income (and principal, if needed for certain living expenses) from Trust B. In addition, he/she will receive all the income from Trust C, and can receive principal, if needed, for certain living expenses.

3. When the surviving spouse dies, the assets in all three trusts are distributed to the beneficiaries.

Advantages

- **Reduce/Eliminate Estate Taxes**—With an A-B-C living trust, you and your spouse can each use your $600,000 federal estate tax exemption. This lets you pass on to your beneficiaries up to $1.2 million estate-tax free and with no probate—saving approximately $235,000 in federal estate taxes, plus probate fees.

- **Provide For Surviving Spouse**—The surviving spouse has complete control over Trust A and receives all income from Trust C. In addition, he/she can receive the income from Trust B and can have access to the principal of Trust B and Trust C, if needed, for certain living expenses.

- **Control For First To Die**—When the first spouse dies and the common trust is divided among Trusts A, B and C, no changes can be made to the provisions of Trust B and Trust C—giving the first spouse to die complete control over who will eventually receive the assets in Trust B and Trust C (half of the common estate).

- **Estate Tax-Free Appreciation Of Trust B**—The value of the assets in Trust B are valued and taxed only when the first spouse dies. There will be no re-valuation or estate taxes paid on any appreciation when the surviving spouse dies and the assets in Trust B are distributed.

- **Estate Taxes Delayed On Trust C**—The assets placed in Trust C are taxed only when the surviving spouse dies. This leaves the estate intact until then, so a larger amount is available to provide income (and principal, if needed) to the surviving spouse during his/her lifetime.

- **Protection Of Assets If Catastrophic Illness Strikes**—In the event of catastrophic illness or injury of the surviving spouse, the trust can be written to protect the assets in Trust B and Trust C—so only the assets in Trust A will need to be "spent down" to qualify for valuable government assistance. However, the income from Trust C will be included in the spouse's assets when application for benefits is made.

Dividing Assets Among Trust A, Trust B And Trust C

The assets are usually divided among Trusts A, B and C after the first spouse dies and the estate tax return is filed. The assets do not have to be liquidated to do this—the allocation can be done "on paper" through bookkeeping. Here again, it is wise to have a professional tax advisor involved to make sure everything is done properly and to maximize your tax planning options.

In The Event Of Catastrophic Illness Or Injury

Unlike the A-B living trust, the surviving spouse *must* receive the income from Trust C. So, if the surviving spouse becomes seriously ill or injured and needs to qualify for government assistance, this income will be considered, along with the assets in Trust A, when application for benefits is made.

However, just as we explained with an A-B living trust, the trustee can be given discretion in deciding whether or not to distribute the income from Trust B, and any principal from Trust B *and* Trust C, to the surviving spouse. This would prevent the assets in Trust B and Trust C from being considered available to pay the surviving spouse's expenses.

Of course, with a sizeable estate, you probably wouldn't spend down the assets in Trust A just to qualify for government benefits—you'd just pay for them yourself. But this can be valuable protection if, after several years, the assets in Trust A have been severely reduced from medical expenses.

SUMMARY—A-B AND A-B-C LIVING TRUSTS

If you are interested in an A-B or an A-B-C living trust, you should consult a qualified estate planning attorney or tax advisor. Depending on your individual situation, he/she may recommend some variations of what we have explained here in order to set up your living trust to best meet your needs and objectives. You may also want to look at a federal estate tax return (available from any IRS office) to see how an estate is taxed, how the exemptions are determined, and how the Q-TIP (Trust C) is filed as part of the marital deduction.

What About Using A Trust In A Will For Tax Planning?

A trust in a will does not avoid probate

The same kinds of tax planning we have described in this section can also be done with a trust in a will—*but you do not avoid probate*. Remember, all wills—even those with trusts in them—must go through probate. A trust in a will can not go into effect until *after* the will has been probated. And by that time, a portion of the estate is lost to probate costs—not to mention all the other problems that go along with probate. With an A-B or A-B-C living trust, you can reduce taxes—*and avoid probate*.

Additional Tax Planning With Irrevocable Options

If your estate is sizeable, you may need additional tax planning beyond an A-B or A-B-C living trust. If so, you may be interested in some of the options explained in Part Five. We have separated these from this discussion because they are *irrevocable* options (you can't change them after you have signed the document). The options in Part Five do not *replace* your living trust—they are *in addition to* it. Your living trust is the foundation of your entire estate plan.

Part Four

PLANNING FOR YOUR LIVING TRUST

Part Four— PLANNING FOR YOUR LIVING TRUST

Your living trust can be designed to include just about anything you want. It is extremely flexible and gives you a lot of control over what will happen to your possessions and to you if you become physically or mentally incapacitated and when you die. But that also means you will need to make some important decisions.

In this section, we will prompt you to think about your individual situation and provide you with information and examples so you can make sound, informed decisions. We'll discuss options for who should be your trustee and back-up trustee(s), how to give your property to your beneficiaries, and special provisions you may want as part of your living trust plan. We'll also help you find the right attorney to prepare your living trust for you.

Now, let's start thinking about your living trust.

YOU MUST MAKE SOME BASIC DECISIONS

What do you want to happen to you and to your assets if you should become incapacitated and when you die? Here are some of the specific things you need to think about and decide:

- Who do you want to take care of you and who do you want to manage your financial affairs if you become incapacitated?

- If you become disabled, do you have specific requests about your medical care?
- Who do you want to distribute your property when you die?
- Who do you want to receive your property and personal belongings?
- Do you want to leave something to your church, favorite charity or foundation?
- If you have minor children, who do you want to manage their inheritance if you and/or your spouse become incapacitated or die?
- Who do you want to raise your children if you are unable to?
- When do you want your children to receive their inheritance?
- Do you have a dependent child, parent or spouse with special needs who will require special care?
- If there are stepchildren in your family, how do you want them to inherit?
- Are there any persons you want to disinherit?
- If your entire family dies before you, who would you want to have your property?
- If you have pets, who do you want to take care of them?

You may have some special instructions if you become incapacitated—for example, you may want certain assets liquidated before others, or you may wish to be cared for in a specific hospital or nursing home (or there may be one you want to avoid).

These are just suggestions. No doubt you will think of others. As you do, it's a good idea to write your ideas down on your Personal and Financial Organizer and discuss them with your attorney. He/she will know if this information should be included in your trust document or if it belongs in a separate letter to your back-up trustees and family.

By the way, along with how you want your property distributed, one of the most valuable things you can do for your back-up trustee(s) and family is to prepare a list of where your property, accounts and papers are located so they will know where to find them.

WHO WILL BE YOUR TRUSTEE?

You can be your own trustee or name someone else

As we mentioned earlier, you can be your own trustee, which is what many people choose to do, especially if their estate is smaller and the trust provisions are fairly simple. This way, nothing changes after you set up your trust—you continue to manage your property and financial affairs (just as you always have) for as long as you are able.

If you are married, you and your spouse can be co-trustees. Most married couples (especially those who have been married for some time) own their property together and are usually very comfortable with this arrangement.

If you and your spouse own some assets separately (for example, property you owned before your marriage or an inheritance), you may want to consider having individual trusts for this property in addition to a common trust for the property you own together. This would keep the property separate, even in community property states.

Of course, you don't have to be your own trustee if you don't want to or if you don't feel qualified. You can name anyone you want as your trustee or to be co-trustee with you—some people choose an adult son or daughter, while many people like having the experience of a corporate trustee (like a bank or trust company—more about this beginning on page 106). This doesn't mean you lose control—you can always change your mind (and your trustee) later.

One big advantage to having a co-trustee is having someone else already involved and familiar with your trust if something happens to you, which would eliminate the time a back-up would have to spend to become knowledgeable with your trust, your beneficiaries and the personalities involved.

If you do decide to name someone as your co-trustee (even your spouse), it might be a good idea to have your trust require both signatures to buy or sell assets as long as both of you are alive and able (just like some bank accounts require both signatures). But if you are concerned that you can't trust this person with your property, he or she probably shouldn't be involved with your trust.

WHO WILL BE YOUR BACK-UP TRUSTEE(S)?

Back-up trustees have a lot of responsibility and should be chosen carefully. Remember, if you (and your co-trustee) become incapacitated, your back-up trustee will step in and take full control for you—paying bills, making financial decisions, even selling or refinancing property. Your back-up will be able to do anything you could with your trust property—as long as it doesn't conflict with the instructions in your trust. And when you die, your back-up acts just like an executor would—takes an inventory of your property, pays your final bills, sells property if necessary, prepares your final tax returns, and distributes your property according to the instructions in your trust.

Who Can Be Back-Up Trustees?

Back-up trustees can be your adult children, other relatives or a trusted friend, and/or a corporate trustee. If you choose an individual, you should name more than one in case your first choice is unable to act. These should be people you know and trust, whose judgment you respect and who will also respect your wishes. They do not have to live in the same state you do (although it would be more convenient if they live close to you).

When choosing your back-ups, keep in mind the type and amount of assets in your trust, the complexity of trust provisions, and the qualifications of those you are considering. Consider personalities, financial/business experience, and time available due to their own family/career demands. Taking over as trustee for someone can take a substantial amount of time and requires a certain amount of business sense.

If you decide to choose one or more of your adult children as your back-ups, you should be prepared for possible hurt feelings if you exclude any—children can be sensitive about these things.

As one solution, some people name all of their adult children to act together as *co*-back-up trustees. Depending on the number of children you have, where they live, and their personalities, this may or may not be a good idea. If you have only two or three children who live in the same area as you (and they get along), then it could work out fine. But you don't want your affairs being run by a cumbersome committee that can't agree on anything. Also, keep in mind

that all their signatures will be required for any transactions—and if they're spread out across the country, that could slow things down.

Choose your back-up trustees carefully

An alternative is to name all of your adult children as back-ups, but instead of having them work together as co-trustees, list them *in order of who you think will do the best job*—and that may not necessarily be oldest to youngest (being older doesn't always make one wiser). So only your first choice would become your back-up, unless he/she is unable or unwilling to serve at that time, in which case the second would step in, and so on down your list.

Having a corporate trustee involved is another option. You may want to consider having a corporate trustee work *with* one or more of your adult children, to get the experience of the corporate trustee and the insight of someone who knows you personally. If you name two of your chidren to act together, you may want to add a corporate trustee as an impartial "third" to prevent any deadlocks if your children disagree (of course, if your children agree, they could not be overruled). You can also name a corporate trustee to act alone.

Make sure you ask your potential back-up trustees if they want this responsibility. Don't put them on the spot and just assume they want to do this. It would probably be helpful for them (and you) to review *Instructions For Back-Up Trustees* on the next two pages. You may also want to give each of your back-ups a copy of this book so they can become familiar with how a living trust works and fully understand the duties and responsibilities of a back-up trustee.

If you have any doubts about a potential back-up trustee's abilities or desire to fulfill this responsibility—if you're not sure about his/her business sense or that he/she may not have the time and/or ability, or if you think this person may act emotionally rather than logically and rationally—you should probably select someone else or a corporate trustee as your back-up.

One final comment. As much as you love your children and would like to think they will be caring and unselfish once you're gone, *this* is the time to be realistic. If they really don't get along, or if there could be jealousies involved, you and your family will probably be much better off if you select a corporate trustee as your back-up. The fee a corporate trustee charges is a small price to pay if it keeps peace in your family.

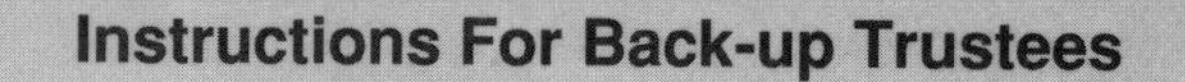

Instructions For Back-up Trustees

If you have been named as back-up trustee for someone, you are probably wondering what you should do when that person dies or becomes incapacitated. This brief checklist will help give you direction at a time when you may not know where to begin. This list will also be helpful if you are deciding who you should name as your back-up trustee.

At Physical Or Mental Incapacity

- Check the trust document for specific instructions. Have the appropriate physician write a letter documenting the person's condition. (Some trust documents will only require a letter from an M.D., others from one or two specialists, etc.)
- Notify the attorney who prepared the trust document. He/she should be aware of the incapacity in case you or family members need to call with questions.
- Notify the bank and others that you are now the trustee for this person. They will probably want to see a copy of the doctor's letter, trust document and your personal identification.
- Secure and inventory any property, especially real estate. Make sure you have keys and take care of any utilities, etc.
- Transact any necessary business for the incapacitated person. You can apply for disability benefits, receive and deposit funds, pay bills (including mortgage and other obligations) and, in general, use the person's assets to take care of him/her until recovery or death.
- Keep a ledger of bills paid and any income received.
- Make sure you keep all back-up trustees fully informed at all times.

At Death

- Inform the family of your position and assist them as needed: funeral arrangements, flowers, cemetery marker, announcement in paper, special wishes for service, notifying friends, relatives, employer, etc.
- Give copies of the trust document to all beneficiaries.
- Make sure you keep all back-up trustees fully informed throughout the process.

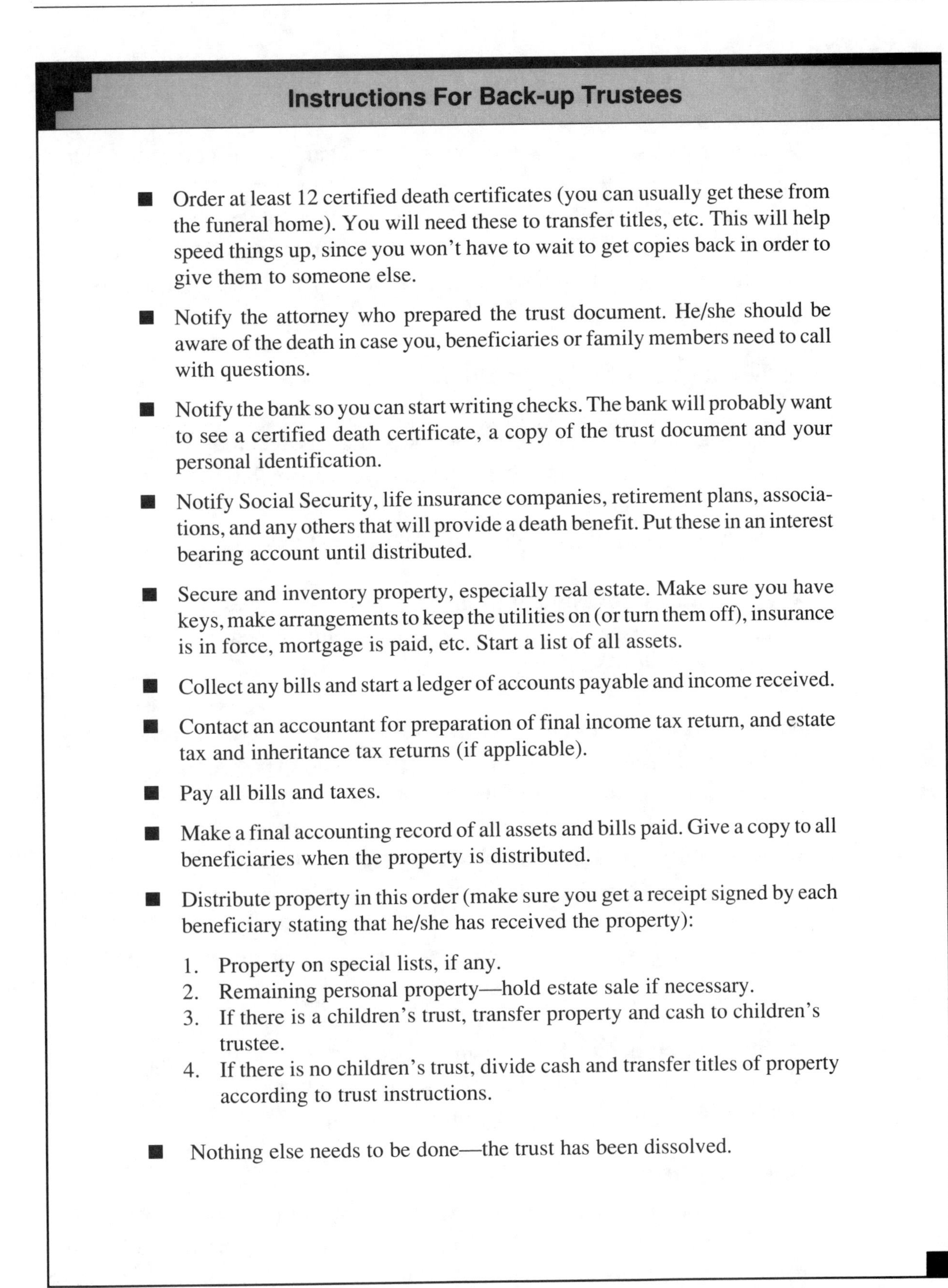

Instructions For Back-up Trustees

- Order at least 12 certified death certificates (you can usually get these from the funeral home). You will need these to transfer titles, etc. This will help speed things up, since you won't have to wait to get copies back in order to give them to someone else.
- Notify the attorney who prepared the trust document. He/she should be aware of the death in case you, beneficiaries or family members need to call with questions.
- Notify the bank so you can start writing checks. The bank will probably want to see a certified death certificate, a copy of the trust document and your personal identification.
- Notify Social Security, life insurance companies, retirement plans, associations, and any others that will provide a death benefit. Put these in an interest bearing account until distributed.
- Secure and inventory property, especially real estate. Make sure you have keys, make arrangements to keep the utilities on (or turn them off), insurance is in force, mortgage is paid, etc. Start a list of all assets.
- Collect any bills and start a ledger of accounts payable and income received.
- Contact an accountant for preparation of final income tax return, and estate tax and inheritance tax returns (if applicable).
- Pay all bills and taxes.
- Make a final accounting record of all assets and bills paid. Give a copy to all beneficiaries when the property is distributed.
- Distribute property in this order (make sure you get a receipt signed by each beneficiary stating that he/she has received the property):

    1. Property on special lists, if any.
    2. Remaining personal property—hold estate sale if necessary.
    3. If there is a children's trust, transfer property and cash to children's trustee.
    4. If there is no children's trust, divide cash and transfer titles of property according to trust instructions.

- Nothing else needs to be done—the trust has been dissolved.

SHOULD I CONSIDER A CORPORATE TRUSTEE?

A corporate trustee is an institution (such as a bank or trust company) which specializes in the management of trusts. Their trained staff of professionals manage the trust assets according to the instructions you put in your trust, handle all required paperwork, maintain accurate records, distribute any income from the trust and, when the trust is dissolved, distribute the assets to your beneficiaries.

Advantages Of A Corporate Trustee:

- **Experience**—They are in the business of trusts, handling many on a daily basis. They are very familiar with the legal responsibilities of a trustee and government requirements, provide excellent records and can handle a variety of trust services economically and efficiently.

- **Professional Investment Management**—They are experienced with all kinds of assets, and many have a variety of investment funds which have performed very well.

- **Regulation**—They are regulated by both state and federal agencies. Also, most courts consider them to be "experts" and expect a higher degree of performance than from an individual.

- **Reliability**—They won't become ill or die, go on vacation, move away or be distracted by personal concerns or emotions (as an individual might).

- **Objectivity**—They will follow your trust instructions objectively and unemotionally.

In addition, corporate trustees are a good source of referrals for estate planning attorneys who are experienced in living trusts. They can also assist you in changing titles, and help you put everything into your trust properly.

No Loss Of Control

If you choose a corporate trustee as your trustee, you still retain control. Until you become incompetent or die, you can always change your trustee if, for any reason, you become unhappy with your choice. And—this is very impor-

tant—even after you become incompetent or die, the trustee you select *must* follow the instructions you put in your trust. In fact, they can be held liable if they don't.

Corporate trustees are in the business of managing trusts

Who Can Benefit From Using A Corporate Trustee

There are many times when a corporate trustee makes an excellent choice as your trustee. The most obvious, of course, is if you are elderly and have no one you can trust to take care of your financial affairs for you—you may be widowed, have no children or other relatives living nearby, or be in declining health. A corporate trustee can give you peace of mind, knowing someone you have personally selected will manage your financial affairs for you now and when you are no longer able to do so yourself.

But there are other times a corporate trustee can be a wise choice. For example, you may not have the time, desire or investment experience to manage your trust yourself. You may travel extensively, or want to spend your time not having to worry about your investments anymore, or feel that someone with more experience could do a better job than you.

You can also have a corporate trustee work with you as *co-trustee*. For example, you may want to take advantage of their investment experience, but still be involved. Or you may want to develop a working relationship now so they will become familiar with your trust and your beneficiaries' needs and personalities while you are alive and competent. This would give you the chance to see how the trustee will perform in your absence, evaluate their investment performance and service, and see if you feel comfortable with them overall (a kind of "trustee test drive").

Of course, not everyone needs a corporate trustee. If you have a modest estate and your trust is fairly simple, you may be just fine being your own trustee and having a capable family member step in for you as your back-up when you are no longer able to manage your trust yourself. But if your estate is larger, has a variety of assets, or if your trust includes tax planning, you would probably be better off having an experienced professional involved.

Remember, too, that family and friends are not always a good choice to be involved with your trust. Even if they do get along, they may be too busy with their own affairs, reside in a distant area or simply not be responsible or experienced enough to manage the trust assets. An innocent error by a well-meaning but inexperienced relative or friend could negate your careful planning and cost your beneficiaries thousands of dollars.

If, after reviewing your situation, you still would like a family member involved (perhaps one or more of your adult children), consider having the two work together. This would give you the advantages of a corporate trustee *and* the personal involvement of someone in your family.

Fees

All trustees are entitled to receive reasonable fees for their services (although you probably won't pay yourself if you are your own trustee and family members rarely accept one). Corporate trustees begin charging a fee *only* when they start to act as trustee for you. Their fees are published and are usually very reasonable, especially when you consider all the services they can provide.

How To Evaluate A Corporate Trustee

If you are considering a corporate trustee, you will want to evaluate them before making a decision. Talk to them. Visit them if you can. Ask how long they have been in business and how many trusts they manage. Compare their investment performance, fees, services they provide and the size of trusts they work with (most have minimum requirements on the size trust they accept, although at some it is as low as $50,000-$100,000—you may have that much in just life insurance). You may want to see samples of the statements and/or reports you would receive. In addition, consider the personalities of the people you meet. And just see how comfortable you feel.

WHO WILL BE YOUR BENEFICIARIES?

As we explained in Part Two, your beneficiaries are the people and/or organizations who will receive your property and possessions when you die. You can leave your belongings to anyone or any organization(s) that you wish. There are, however, some things to keep in mind as you decide when you want your beneficiaries to receive their inheritances. We'll discuss some of your options in the following pages.

If You Have Minor Children

Remember, if you have minor children, your living trust should contain a children's trust to prevent the probate court from taking control of the inheritance.

You will need to name a guardian and trustee for your minor children

Naming A Guardian

You will need to select a guardian for your minor children. This is a very important decision. The person you name will be responsible for raising your children if both parents are dead or incapacitated. Guardians must be adults. You will, of course, want to choose someone who respects your values and standards (moral, ethical and religious) and will raise your children the way you would want. If you want a couple to raise your children, it's a good idea to name one of them as your first choice and the other as your second choice—just in case they were to divorce later.

As we mentioned earlier in Part Two, the court must still officially approve your selection. In most cases, the court will go along with your choice. However, remember that if the other natural parent is still alive, he/she will usually be the court's preferred choice. If you are a single parent with custody and really don't want your "ex" to be guardian, go ahead and name your preference anyway—your choice will, at the very least, receive careful consideration by the court. It's also possible that your "ex" may not be able to take the responsibility (or won't want it). Or the court could agree with you that he/she is not a suitable choice, and would want to know your choice as an alternative.

Naming A Trustee

Remember, the guardian is only responsible for *raising* your children and does not control the inheritance. You need to name a trustee for your children's trust—someone who will be responsible for the safekeeping of their inheritance, and will provide the money for education, medical care, maintenance and other needs from the assets in the children's trust.

Many parents name the same person as trustee and guardian, making it convenient for one person to take care of their children. However, a children's trustee *can* be a different individual, a corporate trustee or, if you wish, you can name two or more to act together as co-trustees. (Depending on the size of the inheritance and type of assets, you may want the benefits of having a

Keep your children's trust flexible

corporate trustee's experience along with the personal insight of a friend or relative.)

One "Common" Trust vs. Separate Trusts

Like most parents, you will want the trust assets to last long enough to provide for each of your children until they reach a certain age (for example, when the last one completes college). To do this, you probably will want to establish *one* children's trust and let the trustee use his/her discretion to provide for each child's individual needs as they arise, just as you would. The remaining assets could be divided after your children are grown.

The alternative—separate trusts for each child with the inheritance split equally among the trusts—has less flexibility. Although this would, on the surface, appear to treat each child equally, it probably would result in *unequal* treatment. First of all, your children are different ages and their needs will last for different lengths of time. For example, the youngest will need to be provided for several years longer than the oldest, and his/her funds could be depleted even before reaching college age—while the oldest one may be able to finish college and have money left over.

Also consider if one child became ill or injured and needed special medical treatment. If you were alive, you wouldn't stop providing for this child's care after you had spent a certain amount of money—you and your other children would probably sacrifice to make sure this child received the treatment he/she needed. But if you create separate trusts for each child, your trustee won't have that option.

Give Your Children's Trustee Flexibility

You may want to give your trustee some flexibility in how to use the trust assets. For example, the guardian(s) may need some extra assistance in providing for your children. Put yourself in the shoes of your children's guardian for a moment—suddenly you have additional children to raise. Is there enough room for everyone in your home, or do you need to add on an extra bedroom? Can you handle the extra workload yourself or do you need to hire a part-time helper? You might even need a larger car!

Caring for your children should not be a financial burden on the person(s) you have asked to be guardian—as long as you have planned and left enough

assets to provide for them adequately. And if you trust your trustee to manage the inheritance, he/she should be able to use good judgment to provide for the necessary comfort and well-being of your children.

By the way, this may be a good time to review your total plan with your insurance agent or financial advisor. Do you realistically have enough assets to provide for your children and/or spouse the way you would want if something happened to you today? Or what if something happened to your spouse—would you have enough to manage without him or her? If you don't have enough assets to provide for your family as you would like to, you may want to increase your life insurance.

Allowing For Loans/Advances For Your Older Children

To make sure the trust assets provide for all your children, you probably will want to keep the trust intact until the youngest child has reached an appropriate age.

But, at the same time, you may not want to penalize your older children who may need funds to help purchase a home, pay for a wedding, start a business, etc. while they are waiting for the youngest to "grow up." You might consider allowing for an advance or loan from their inheritance, which would be subtracted later when the trust assets are distributed. Your trustee should, of course, make sure the advance is appropriate and justified (both in amount and purpose), so that the amount withdrawn from the trust does not adversely affect the other children. You should probably give your trustee some guidelines—such as specifying a limit on the amount of the advance to be considered.

How And When Do You Want Your Adult Children To Inherit?

You have many options for distribution of your children's inheritance once they are adults. One would be to give them the full amount immediately upon your death. But many parents prefer to give their children more than one opportunity to invest or to use their inheritance wisely (which doesn't always happen the first time around).

Here's one option. You could specify that, if your youngest child is age 25 or older when both you and your spouse die, each child would immediately receive one-third of his/her inheritance. One-third would be distributed five years later, and the final third in another five years.

As an alternative, you could specify a percentage at certain ages, but make sure you review your trust regularly. Otherwise, your children could have already passed those ages by the time you die and would receive their inheritance in one lump sum—defeating your intention of distributing it in installments. To prevent this, your trust can specify that if your children have passed these ages, the inheritance would then be payable in installments every so many years (like above).

Be careful about linking the distributions to certain occasions—marriage, birth of the first child, etc. It could be that your child doesn't marry or have children. (This could also encourage an insincere marriage, and part of the inheritance could end up outside the family.)

Using graduation from college as a milestone can also present some potential problems. For example, how would you define "college"—2-year, 4-year, trade school? And what if your son or daughter decides to pursue a career (music, dance, sculpture, etc.) for which a college degree isn't necessary?

Percentages are usually better than amounts, because you don't know what the trust assets will be at that time. Your attorney can provide you with some suggestions on how to best accomplish your objectives. Also, your friends may have some interesting ideas. Always remember that this is *your* plan—make sure you end up with something you want that also meets the needs and maturity of your children.

Providing For An Irresponsible Child

If you feel you have a child who is too irresponsible to receive outright control of his/her inheritance (or one who has a problem with drugs, alcohol, gambling, etc.), you can specify that the inheritance remain "in trust" for your child's lifetime or until he/she reaches a more mature age. The trustee will manage and invest the inheritance, and provide for your child's needs. (This is an excellent situation for a corporate trustee.)

A spendthrift clause, which protects the trust assets from creditors, is also a good idea. This provision states that the beneficiary cannot voluntarily dispose of any trust assets or income before they are paid to him/her. So if, for example, your irresponsible son or daughter buys an expensive sports car, the trust cannot be held responsible for payment.

You'll also need to specify who will receive any remaining inheritance if your son or daughter dies before receiving the full amount.

Grandparents should set up a trust for grandchildren

If You Have Stepchildren

If you have stepchildren, you will need to decide how you want them to inherit—or if you want them to inherit from you at all. This can be a delicate situation, but you will need to discuss it openly and frankly with your spouse.

If You Have Grandchildren

Grandparents can also set up a children's trust to leave assets to grandchildren. You don't have to set up a separate trust—the children's trust can be included in your living trust. You can be the trustee, and you will also need to name a back-up trustee (perhaps one or both parents and/or a corporate trustee). The trust will continue until all of the children have reached the age(s) you want them to receive their inheritances. You can also specify how you want them to inherit—just as we explained above. Whatever you do, don't leave anything directly to your minor grandchildren—you don't want to cause a probate guardianship.

If the inheritance is substantial, you should be aware that a generation skipping transfer tax may be involved. (See Part Five for more information.)

Providing For Disabled Children (Special Needs Trust)

If you have a child who is physically, mentally or developmentally disabled—from birth, illness, injury or drug abuse—he/she may be entitled to government benefits (Supplemental Security Income and/or Medicaid) now or in the future. However, most of these benefits are available only to those with very minimal assets.

Like many parents, you may find yourself faced with a difficult choice—if you leave a substantial inheritance to this child, he/she will be disqualified from receiving the government benefits which may be crucial for his/her care. On the other hand, you may not want to have to disinherit this child in order to preserve these benefits.

There is a third option. With a separate trust (a special needs trust), you can provide for your disabled child without interfering with his/her benefits. (This trust can be established at the same time as your living trust.) This trust should be very specific in stating that its purpose is to *supplement* government

Providing for a disabled child takes special planning

benefits—that is, to provide only benefits or luxuries *above and beyond* the benefits the child receives from any local, state, federal or private agencies.

It is extremely important that the trust not duplicate any government-provided services and that the child not have any resemblance of ownership of the trust assets. Otherwise, it is very possible that the government would attempt to seize the trust assets for repayment of services provided or determine that the child does not qualify for future benefits because he or she has ample assets and income to provide for adequate care.

To make sure the child does not have any implied ownership in the trust assets, the trust should give the trustee complete control over the distribution of the assets and any income they generate—your child should not be able to demand any principal or interest from the trust. You should also instruct the trustee to purchase only goods and services that government benefits do not provide—such as airline tickets to visit relatives, furniture, stereo, etc. (The trustee should make the purchase direct, instead of giving the money to the child and letting the child make the purchase.) A spendthrift clause is also a good idea for extra protection.

Who should be trustee? Of course, you can be trustee while you are alive (you and your spouse can be co-trustees). But someone will need to assume this responsibility after your death (or incompetency), so you will need to name a back-up trustee.

The most obvious choice is another family member or close personal friend who has a deep concern for the child's welfare. This may be one or more of your healthy adult children. As with any back-up trustee, be sure to discuss this with the person(s) you have in mind. Make sure they have the time, ability and desire to take on this responsibility. Also, be aware of a possible conflict of interest, especially if your other children will inherit the trust after your disabled child has died—they may be more interested in preserving the trust assets than in putting the disabled child's needs first.

This is an excellent situation for a corporate trustee, especially if you do not want to burden other family members with this responsibility or don't want to worry about a possible conflict of interest. And, of course, you don't have to worry about your child outliving the corporate trustee—they'll be around to provide for the child's needs for as long as he/she lives.

You may want to consider a blend of the two—for example, the corporate trustee can manage the assets and a relative can be responsible for determining and purchasing the goods and services which will make the child more comfortable. You may also want to consider having a corporate trustee work with you now—to take advantage of their investment skills and to have them become familiar with the child and his/her needs.

How much should you put into the trust? Among other things, you will want to take into consideration how long you expect your child to live, the kind of care he/she will need, the benefits available (now and projected), how much interest the assets can be expected to generate, how much you can afford to put into the trust, and how much you want to give to other beneficiaries.

As you can see, providing for a disabled child takes more thought and is more complicated than providing for your other children. *Make sure* you use an attorney who has experience in setting up special needs trusts for disabled children—standard beneficiary wording just will not do.

Special Note: If you have other disabled dependents (perhaps a parent, grandparent, brother, sister, etc.) you want to care for, you can follow these same general guidelines. Again, make sure you discuss this in detail with an attorney who has experience in these areas.

Distribution Per Capita Or Per Stirpes?

Read your trust document carefully. There may be some legal phrases with which you may not be familiar.

In the distribution section, you should specifically look for *per capita* or *per stirpes*. These phrases are used to specify how your descendents will receive your property when one or more of your immediate beneficiaries dies before you—in other words, if one of your children dies before you do, how his/her children (and your other living children) will inherit.

This is confusing at first, especially if you have trouble following family trees. But it is very important to understand these because they distribute the property very differently. So take it slowly and follow along with the flow charts.

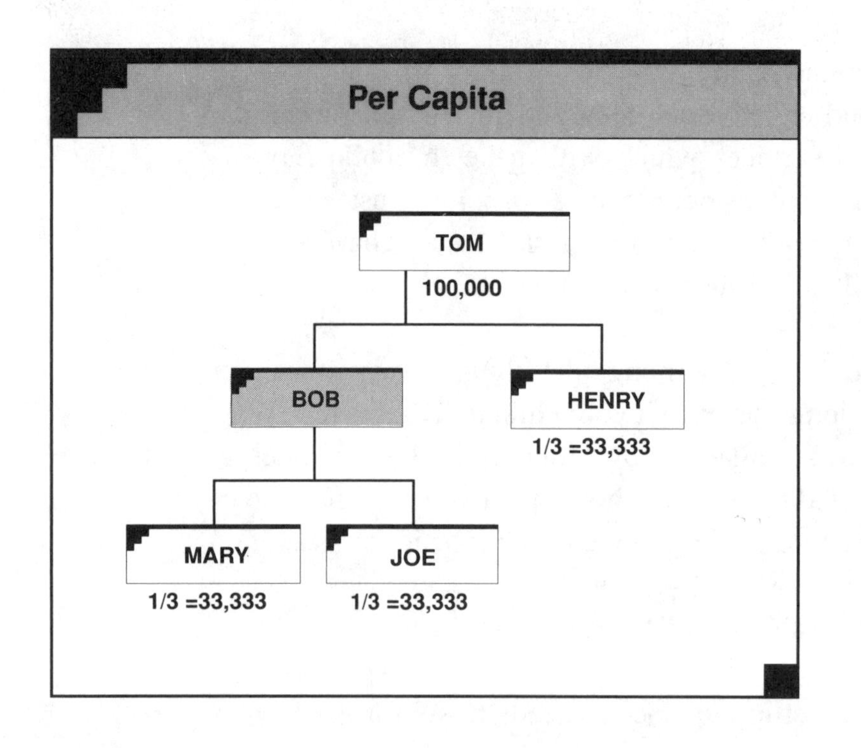

Distribution per capita (or *by pro rata* or *share and share alike*) means that the surviving descendents will receive equal shares of the inheritance, regardless of generation. Let's say Tom, a widower, has two grown sons—Bob and Henry. Bob dies before his father Tom. Henry and his brother's two children (Tom's grandchildren—Mary and Joe) will each receive one-third of Tom's estate.

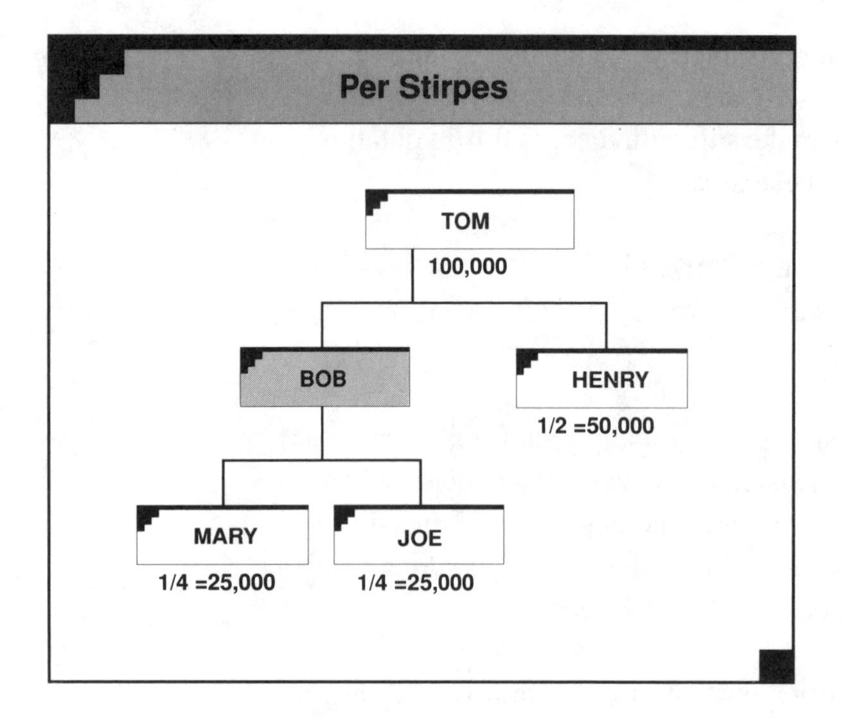

Distribution per stirpes (or *by representation*) means that your surviving descendents will only receive what their immediate ancestor would receive. Using the same example, Henry will receive 50% of his father's estate. Bob's children (Mary and Joe) will each receive 25% of their grandfather's estate, splitting the 50% their father would have received.

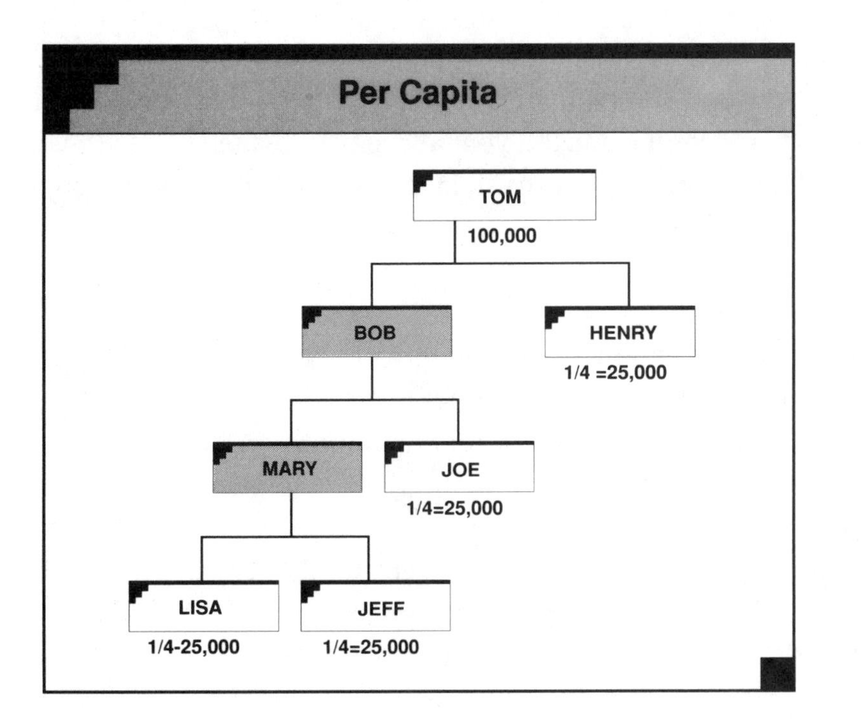

Now let's carry this a generation further. Let's say that Bob's daughter Mary, who had two children (Lisa and Jeff), also dies before her grandfather. When Tom dies, under the *per capita* instructions his four beneficiaries—son Henry, grandson Joe and greatgrandchildren Lisa and Jeff—will each receive one-fourth of his estate.

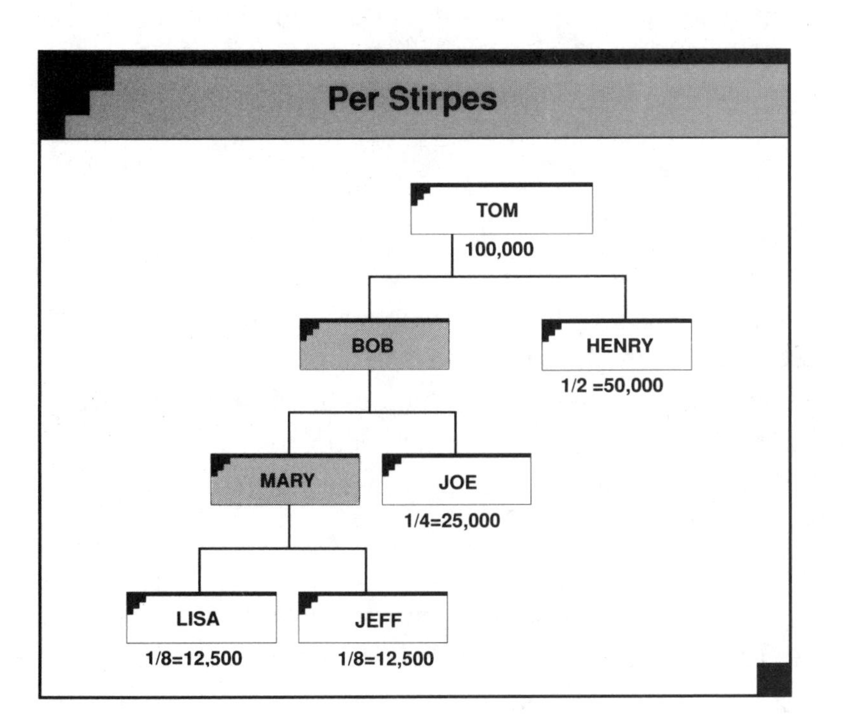

However, under *per stirpes* instructions, Mary's children would split the inheritance their mother would have received. Henry receives 50%, Mary's brother Joe receives 25% and Mary's two children will each receive 12.5% (splitting Mary's share).

As a general reminder, if there is anything in your trust document you don't understand, ask your attorney to explain it to you until you do understand it. And if it's something you don't want, tell your attorney to change it. As we've already said several times—this is *your* trust. Don't be too embarrassed or shy to make sure it is everything you want.

Alternate Beneficiaries

You should think about who you would want to have your property if all of the people you have named as your beneficiaries die before you. Many people specify their church, a favorite charity, or foundation.

Disinheriting

Are there any relatives you specifically do not want to inherit from you? This could be a touchy subject, but if you have strong feelings about this and it's important to you, it should be included in your living trust.

Special Gifts

You probably will want to leave specific items to certain individuals or organizations—a favorite piece of jewelry or antique that you want to give to a special friend or relative. These are called your "Special Gifts" or "Special Bequests."

As we explained in Part Two, you can do this very easily by preparing a "Special Gifts List" and having it notarized. You don't need a special form to do this. Just use a piece of paper and write down who will receive a special gift and what you are giving to them. You may want to make a separate list for each person or organization, so as you make changes or additions you won't have to re-do the entire list. Remember, you can keep your list at home and add to it or change it at any time. Just make sure you date each list and always have the new list notarized.

To avoid any family disagreements when you die, make your lists as specific as you can. You don't need to list every single item (like each piece of silverware or item of clothing), but make sure you list items of real or sentimental value. It's much easier for you to do this yourself than to expect your children and other relatives to reach an agreement which satisfies everyone. Otherwise, family disagreements could still prompt an estate sale.

Giving To Charities, Churches And Foundations

This is an excellent time to think about giving to a favorite charity or foundation. Take a few minutes to think about organizations or causes that are special to you—some national, perhaps international, and some local. There are many excellent ones, and they are all in need of funding to continue their work. There is sure to be one or more that you would like to help. In addition to the tax benefits of charitable donations, you have the power to do something good, to express yourself—to put something of value back into the world.

100% of your gift will go to the organization you specify

For example, you may have been very active in your church, synagogue, or other religious, fraternal or charitable organization—perhaps it provided support to you at a critical time in your life—and you would like to return the support. Maybe someone very close to you died from cancer, Alzheimer's or another disease, and you would like to help fund research to find a cure. Many people give in the memory of a loved one. You may feel very strongly about education, the hungry and homeless, protecting the environment, world peace, animal rights, the arts, organ donation—the list of worthwhile causes is endless.

Your gift can be as specific or as general, as large or as small, as you want to make it. You could set up a scholarship program for underprivileged children, buy new chairs or religious textbooks for your church or synagogue, or help fund a building project. The charity or foundation of your choice will be glad to make suggestions and help you set up your gift program. Some may even be able to recommend an attorney who specializes in living trusts.

Giving is very easy with a living trust. With a living trust you can be sure your wishes are carried out—unlike a will, which is often contested by the heirs to prevent charitable donations. And because there are no probate costs or delays, 100% of your gift will immediately go to the charity or foundation of your choice.

Special Note:

Make sure you specify the legal name and the location (including address) of the organization you want to receive the gift. For example, if you want the local office of a national organization to have it, make sure you clearly state so—otherwise, the local office and the national office could end up fighting each other in court to see who will receive the gift.

Also, if you are unsure whether or not the organization will be around to receive the gift, list an alternate charitable beneficiary. Otherwise, the gift will probably end up in court, and the court will have to decide who will ultimately receive it.

In Part Five, we discuss some of the ways you can give to a charity or foundation so you (or your estate) will receive special tax advantages.

PUTTING EXTRA PROTECTION IN YOUR LIVING TRUST

As we've said several times, everything should be included in your living trust if you want to completely avoid probate. You should change titles and beneficiary designations as soon as possible after your living trust document has been completed. However, something may happen to prevent you from changing all of them, or you may inadvertently forget one. For maximum protection (and convenience), your living trust "plan" should include the following provisions.

Statement Of Your Intentions

First, there should be a "special" section in your living trust document stating that it is your *intention* that all of your property (titled and untitled, including your personal belongings) be included in your living trust, *unless you specifically exclude a certain property in writing*. It should also give your back-up trustee(s) special additional powers, giving them the very specific authority to change the titles of any forgotten property to the name of your trust. This section should be separately signed and notarized, so it could be recorded if necessary.

These powers should automatically apply to the back-up trustee who steps in for you—it should go with the trustee position, rather than being limited to a specific individual. This way, if your first choice for back-up trustee is unable to take over for you, your second choice (or third, if necessary) will have this authority. The instructions should be very specific—your back-up can *only* transfer titles to the name of your trust. This way you won't have to worry about your back-up trustee being able to change the titles to anything other than your trust. You have already stated that you *intended* for all of your property to be in your trust—you are simply giving your back-up trustee the power to carry out these instructions.

The intention, of course, is to make it impossible for anything you own to have to go through probate. *There is no guarantee this will work*—that decision will vary from court to court and will depend on the value and type of property or assets. But the legal theory is that your back-up trustee could transfer titles *after* your death, and *before* probate proceedings can start. *This does not (and should never) take the place of changing titles and beneficiary designations when your trust is set up and as you accumulate additional property.*

Pour Over Will—Another Safety Net

As additional protection, your trust should include a "pour over will," stating that anything you may have inadvertently left out of your living trust will go into it at your death. This is an extra precaution in case the special paragraph discussed above is not accepted by the court. If this happens, the "forgotten" property will probably have to be probated, but at least your pour over will "catches" the property and sends it back into your living trust. The property will then be distributed as part of your living trust plan.

Here's another reason to have a pour over will. In some states, the guardian for minor children must be named in a will. So if you have a children's trust in your living trust, your attorney will also include the guardian in your pour over will to satisfy this requirement.

Power Of Attorney—For Convenience

The third component is a power of attorney (or a durable power of attorney if your state permits it). As we said earlier, both of these end at death, but a durable power of attorney will still be valid if you become physically or mentally incapacitated. (See page 21 or *Definitions* at the back of the book.)

Either power of attorney (regular or durable) has a value when combined with your living trust. The power of attorney should be given to the same people you name as your back-up trustees (and co-trustee if you have one) and in the same order. This will allow the power of attorney to automatically transfer to the back-up who steps in for you, and it also keeps these special powers concentrated with just your back-up trustees.

This is mainly for convenience. Although your living trust gives authority to your back-up trustee (or to your spouse if named as co-trustee) to act for you, many people and institutions (such as hospitals and nursing homes) may not be that familiar with living trusts. Rather than trying to educate them in an emergency, you can simply show them your power of attorney which is readily recognized by just about everyone. In these situations, a power of attorney is actually more appropriate than showing someone your living trust document. Besides, you will probably consider your living trust plan private and you may not feel comfortable having to show it to strangers.

If your state permits a durable power of attorney, it can be even more helpful. Your durable power of attorney should include another special paragraph, giving your back-ups (in order of succession) not only the regular power to sign your name, but also the additional power to re-title any forgotten property from your name to the name of your trust. This way, if you become incapacitated and your back-up trustee finds that you forgot to put a piece of property into your trust, he/she will easily be able to change the title and put it into your trust for you.

Even if your state does not permit a durable power of attorney, this paragraph should be used with a regular power of attorney. Your back-up trustee will not be able to use it if you are incompetent. But if you are well and simply out of the country or otherwise unavailable, your back-up can conveniently use it to re-title property and put it into your trust for you.

These Are Only Extra Precautions

These are a combination of three very reliable and long proven legal concepts—a living trust, a will and a power of attorney. However, these extra safety nets *do not take the place of changing titles and beneficiary designations to your trust while you are alive and able. Don't put off completing your trust* thinking that these provisions will do it for you. Nothing can guarantee an assignment of all of your property to your trust if *you* don't change the titles.

Certificate of Trust

As you begin changing titles, some institutions may insist upon having a copy of or reviewing your trust so they will know it is valid. For example, your bank will probably want verification of your trust before changing your accounts, safe deposit box, etc. But you may not want them to see your entire trust document, and legally you are under no obligation to furnish anyone with a copy of your trust.

An alternative is to have your attorney prepare a *Certificate of Trust* for you. This is a shortened version of your trust that will usually satisfy these requests. It verifies the existence of your trust, explains the powers given to the trustee, identifies the back-up trustees, etc., but it does not reveal any of your confidential information (such as your assets and your beneficiaries). Your attorney may call it by another name, but he/she will probably know what needs to be prepared.

Living Will

You may want to consider a living will. This is a simple document that lets your physician know the kind of life support treatment you would want if you were to become terminally ill or injured with no hope for recovery. The wording for a living will is short and standard—you can get a copy of one from your attorney, doctor, hospital, or nursing/medical association.

However, while the purpose of a living will is honorable, you should be aware that it may or may not do what you expect it to do. In some states, the document is binding—if a doctor or hospital refuses to honor a living will, they must withdraw from the case. But in other states, it is not legally binding on anyone—it is simply a "directive" to your physician. Many doctors and hospitals are reluctant to discontinue any life sustaining treatment (remember, they have been trained to *save* lives). And if someone objects to the instructions in your living will, it's almost certain the doctor and hospital will not follow through as you have requested—most just don't want to be held liable.

Also, a living will is a *statutory* document—the wording is very specific and limited (it only addresses the use of life support under very specific conditions) and can't be altered or personalized.

Durable Power Of Attorney For Health Care

A durable power of attorney for health care, where available, is usually preferred because it is more broad and binding than a living will. This document gives legal authority to another person to make any health care decisions for you (including the use of life support) in the event you are unable to make them for yourself—which can be very valuable if you need surgery or medical treatment of any kind. You can also specify in this document the kind of life support treatment you would want in a terminal situation.

Check with your attorney to see if a durable power of attorney for health care (or similar document) is available in your state. You should also talk with your doctor about your feelings on this subject and find out how he/she feels about a durable power of attorney for health care and living wills. (If your doctor is not supportive of your view, you may want to find one who is.)

HOW TO FIND THE RIGHT ATTORNEY FOR YOUR LIVING TRUST

You will need to find an estate planning attorney who believes in living trusts and does them regularly. The best way to do this, of course, is through a personal referral from someone who has had a living trust done. Ask your friends, banker, trust company, CPA, investment broker, financial planner, family or business attorney, church/synagogue, or charity if they can recommend an attorney who is experienced in living trusts.

Here's another excellent source of referrals. The American College of Trust and Estate Counsel (formerly The American College of Probate Counsel) is an elite association of over 2,600 lawyers and law professors who have extensive experience in estate planning. To qualify for membership as a "fellow," a candidate must have at least ten years active practice in probate and trust law or estate planning, an "outstanding reputation, exceptional skill and substantial contributions to the field by lecturing, writing, teaching and participating in bar activities." To receive a list of members in your city, you can write to the following address. (If you live outside a metropolitan area, be sure to include the city closest to you.)

The American College of Trust and Estate Counsel
2716 Ocean Park Blvd., Suite 1080
Santa Monica, California 90405
(Requests are handled by mail only.)

You will want to get several recommendations and interview each attorney to find one with whom you are comfortable and you feel is best qualified for your situation. You can shop by phone, or in many cities you can now attend living trust seminars.

You want the best value—not the cheapest price

Here are some questions you will want to ask and things to keep in mind:

1. Tell the attorney you want a basic living trust document that will keep your family out of probate when you die or if you become incapacitated. Be suspicious of an attorney who tries to talk you out of a living trust and wants to talk you into a will or joint ownership. Think again if the attorney tries to convince you that a living trust is complicated and expensive. Remember, most living trust documents are standardized and do not normally require much modification to take care of most people's needs.

2. Ask the attorney how many living trusts he/she has done. How much experience does the attorney have in this area? Can he/she provide you with any references, such as a bank, trust company, CPA? You don't need to pay for educating your attorney about living trusts.

   If the attorney has done a number of living trusts, he or she will be much more efficient and knowledgeable, and will save you time and money. Plus, you'll feel confident that your living trust is done correctly.

3. Ask how the attorney charges for living trusts and what payment procedure he/she uses. Many attorneys charge by the hour, while those who specialize in living trusts will usually have a flat rate.

   Ask about any charges that are additional—such as transferring property into your trust. Briefly describe your situation, then ask the attorney to give you a "ballpark" cost estimate in advance. (Remember, if your situation is complicated or if you need tax planning, you will probably pay more.) Be wary if an attorney is reluctant to talk about pricing.

   Don't be afraid or embarrassed to shop around and compare prices. But, at the same time, be careful not to sacrifice quality for price. You want the best *value*—not the cheapest price.

Think of a living trust as a service instead of a product

4. Where is the attorney located? You want to deal with someone who is convenient. Does he/she have extended office hours? Is the office open on weekends? You don't want to take time away from work if you have a choice.

5. Ask about the procedure and how long is required to complete your living trust plan. Once you've made your decisions (who you want as trustee, your back-ups, beneficiaries, etc.), the attorney should be able to provide you with a first draft of the documents within a couple of weeks. It may take another couple of weeks for you to review them and have any corrections made. How long it will actually take will depend on how quickly you can respond, how complicated your trust is, and how busy your attorney is.

   If the attorney says he/she can do your trust in a day or two, be careful. Maybe your trust is so simple and the attorney is so well organized he/she can provide you with a good trust that quickly. But, at the same time, you want to make sure the attorney spends enough time with you to understand your situation and concerns.

   Think of this as a *service* instead of a *product*—you don't just walk into an attorney's office and buy a trust like you would a box of cereal from the grocery store.

6. Can you go in for a free consultation? The attorney should be willing to spend 20-30 minutes with you at no charge to answer your general questions.

7. Personalities and confidence are important. Your attorney should be someone you are comfortable with, someone you can talk to, and someone who seems to be genuinely interested in you and your family's welfare. Does the attorney seem willing to answer your questions, or do you feel that you are only taking up his/her time? Your attorney should encourage you to ask questions and voice your concerns.

8. When you go in for your free consultation, look around at the attorney's office. Is it neat and clean? Does the attorney appear to be well-organized?

9. Take this book and your completed Personal and Financial Organizer with you and show it to the attorney. Be suspicious if the attorney tries to downplay the information and discourage you from wanting to stay out of probate. The attorney you want to deal with should endorse any information which correctly explains living trusts and helps you avoid probate.

10. Ask to see a sample of the documents you will receive. A complete trust plan will usually include more than the living trust document—look for a pour over will, a durable power of attorney and durable power of attorney for health care (or a regular power of attorney and the option of a living will if these are not available in your state).

    The documents themselves should be well organized and easy to follow. Look for numbered paragraphs, headings, perhaps a table of contents. See if you can read and understand them—if the actual documents are written in legalese, there should be a summary written for the lay person. Some attorneys package all of the documents in a binder, with a table of contents, divided sections, and a summary of each document in simple English.

    The way the documents are written and organized will be a good reflection of the type of work the attorney does.

11. How much assistance does the attorney provide you in changing titles and beneficiary designations to your trust? Does the attorney automatically do this for you? Is there an additional charge? (Even if there is, it's usually worth the cost to save you time and make sure everything is done properly.) Or does the attorney just do the documents and leave this part of the process completely up to you?

    Many times the attorney will include pre-written letters you can send to your bank, savings and loan, etc. with instructions for changing titles (these are very helpful). How much assistance the attorney gives you is usually another good indication of the quality of work he/she does.

Living Trust Seminars

With the growing popularity of living trusts, some attorneys are conducting seminars explaining living trusts—usually at no charge. This is an excellent way to learn more about living trusts and to see the attorney "in action" from a distance.

It's also a good opportunity to ask questions (and hear other people's questions) and evaluate the attorney. Does the attorney seem to know what he/she is talking about? Can you understand the presentation? How well does the attorney answer questions? Does the attorney give you something to take home and read? Is the presentation (and the materials) professionally done?

Usually, the attorney will stay after the seminar to meet the attendees, answer individual questions, and schedule appointments. Some even give a discount off the price of a trust if you attend the seminar, which is good for both of you—the attorney saves time by explaining the basics to several people at one time and you save money on your trust. If you are interested in attending one of these seminars, check your local newspaper for advertisements or listen to a local "talk radio" station.

If you do attend a seminar, remember that the quality of the seminar is only part of it. In the end, what counts is the quality of the trust documents the attorney prepares for you.

Prepaid Legal Services Plans

One way to get your living trust done at a reasonable cost may be through one of the group or prepaid legal services plans. These are becoming very popular and growing quickly all across the country, with many employers, associations and unions offering them to their employees and members. Several are also being offered direct to the public through credit cards. You should check to see if you qualify for membership in one—it could save you a lot of time and money on your living trust and on other legal matters.

Under these plans, some legal services are free—such as review of legal documents, and telephone and office consultations. (This is an ideal free way to learn about their living trust services or ask questions about your trust once it is set up.) Other services are offered at discounts and usually there is a limit on the attorney's hourly rate. Some of these plans are national, so if you move to a new state you can have your trust reviewed at little or no cost.

Most of these plans use local attorneys to provide the services. You will still need to personally interview attorneys (just as we've explained) until you find an estate planning attorney who is experienced in living trusts and with whom you feel comfortable.

Finding the right attorney is very important

If you are interested in finding a prepaid legal services plan, you can contact the American Prepaid Legal Services Institute and they can tell you which prepaid plans are available in your state. The American Bar Association is one of its supporters. Here is their address:

The American Prepaid Legal Services Institute
750 North Lake Shore Drive
Chicago, IL 60611

The Actual Process

Once you've found the right attorney for you, this is what should happen.

1. Take your completed Personal and Financial Organizer to your initial attorney interview. Or better yet, mail a copy to the attorney in advance, so he/she has time to review it before your meeting. The attorney will review your information, discuss it with you, answer your questions and probably make some suggestions for you to consider. Make sure you get a definite cost from the attorney at this point.

2. The attorney will prepare a draft of the living trust document for you to review and approve. Make sure you read it carefully and be sure you understand everything. Don't be afraid to ask questions.

3. After you have approved the draft, the final trust document will be prepared for signing. This means you (and your spouse) will sign it, and it will be notarized. Usually there are two original documents—so if by some chance you misplace one, you will have another original. If your attorney is using a simple pour over will and power of attorney with your living trust, these will be signed and notarized at this time.

4. Titles and appropriate beneficiary designations will then need to be changed from your name to the name of your living trust.

Remember, getting a living trust is just the first step (although it's a big step). Your living trust plan is not complete until all titles and appropriate beneficiary designations have been changed. While your attorney will probably provide some assistance, it is your responsibility to make sure this happens.

Changing Titles and Beneficiary Designations

Your attorney will probably transfer the title of your home for you as part of the cost of your living trust. In addition, he/she should also help you change other titles and beneficiary designations—or at least give you information on how to do this.

But if not, you can change them yourself, dealing directly with your bank or trust officer, savings and loan, credit union, employee benefits department, insurance agent, financial planner, CPA, etc. Just check with your attorney for the exact wording you should use.

As you will see, most of these are not difficult to do—**you just have to take the time to do it**. Remember, your living trust is not complete until you transfer your assets into it—anything you leave out will probably have to be probated. Remember, too, that anything you put into your trust can always be taken out at a later date. You do not lose control of your property—you continue to buy and sell property just as you did before.

We have included the most common types of property people own. If you own something not included here, be sure to ask your attorney how to put it into your trust.

Your Home, Real Estate, Land, Condominium, Etc.

These are all considered "real property." To put these into your trust, you will need to transfer the title from your name (exactly as it is worded on the original) to the name of your trust. For example, from "John and Mary Smith, husband and wife" to "John and Mary Smith, Trustees under trust dated January 1, 1990."

Depending on the state in which the property is located, you will use a correction deed or quitclaim to do this (you can also use a warranty or grant deed). Each deed will need to be notarized and recorded in the county where the property is located, including any out-of-state property you own.

The attorney who prepares your trust document will probably automatically transfer your home to your living trust for you. For an additional charge, he/

she will probably change other real estate titles for you if you wish. Remember, in most cases this will not trigger a re-assessment of the property taxes or disturb the current mortgage in any way.

Your living trust is not complete until you transfer your assets into it

Mortgages/Loans You Owe

Setting up a living trust will not normally affect any mortgages or notes you owe, so you don't need to do anything with these. You just continue making your required payments as usual.

Mortgages/Loans Owed To You

If you have "owner-financed" property, loaned someone money or have any other notes payable to you, you will need to *assign* these mortgages/loans to your living trust. This is done by a separate assignment which is signed by you only (not the other party), notarized and attached to the original mortgage/note. Additional signatures and recordings are not required.

Checking Accounts

All bank checking accounts should be in the name of your trust. To do this, just the signature card needs to be corrected, showing your living trust as the "owner." Only the trustee(s) should be authorized to sign checks, and no one but your bank needs to know this is a trust account. Your checks do not need to be changed unless you want to—they can still be printed with just your name, address and telephone number on them—and you continue to sign checks the same way you always have. Your bank may want to see a copy of the trust document—if so, a Certificate of Trust (discussed earlier in Part Four), may satisfy their requirements.

Savings Accounts

These should be retitled in the name of your trust. If a beneficiary designation is permitted, it should also be your trust. An officer at your bank or savings and loan can assist you.

Certificates of Deposit

These should be retitled in the name of your trust and, if permitted, the beneficiary designation should also be your trust. You do not need to cash these in to do this. Some holders (bank, etc.) will retitle the certificates immediately. If yours requires you to wait until the certificate matures, you can go ahead and change the beneficiary designation now and, by using a separate document, assign your ownership interest to your trust. Then, when the certificate matures, you can change the title before you renew it.

Stocks/Bonds/Mutual Funds

If you maintain an account in the name of your bank or brokerage company (called a "street account") or invest in a mutual fund, just notify your banker, broker or mutual fund to change the name on your account. (They will probably want instructions in writing from you.)

If you have possession of actual stock and securities certificates, you will need to have new certificates issued in the name of your trust. Never write or mark on an original stock or bond certificate. Contact your broker or banker for assistance.

Life Insurance Policies

If you are single and the total value of your estate is less than $600,000 or if you are married and it is less than $1.2 million, you need to change the beneficiary designations and ownership (of those you own) to your living trust. Your insurance agent can provide the proper forms. If your estate is greater than this, you should consider an irrevocable life insurance trust (see Part Five).

Deferred Savings Plans

These would include your IRA, retirement/savings plans (like a 401(k)), pension plan, Keogh, and other tax-deferred plans. You probably won't be able to change the ownership of these to your living trust, but your living trust can be beneficiary. However, as we discussed in Part Two, if you are married you may decide to name your spouse as the first beneficiary and your living trust as second (alternate) beneficiary for tax reasons. You and your spouse should discuss your options together and with your own personal tax advisor.

To change the beneficiary designation on employer-sponsored plans, contact your employee benefits or personnel department for the proper form. To change the beneficiary on your IRA, you will need to contact the establishment which "holds" your IRA for you (bank, savings and loan, etc.).

Other Employer-Provided Benefits

These would include life insurance, accident insurance and other plans your employer provides for you. Usually, your employer owns the plan, but your trust should be the beneficiary when you have this option. Your employee benefits or personnel department will have the appropriate forms and can help you complete them.

Safe Deposit Box

The box authorization card should be changed to the name of your trust so your back-up trustee can have ready access at your death or incompetency. Only the trustee(s) will need to sign the card to do this. Your bank or savings and loan officer can help you do this.

Automobiles/Boats/Other Vehicles

Most states will permit a vehicle title to be re-issued in the name of a trust. In some states, however, this will require the payment of an excise (transfer) tax, just as if the trust had purchased it. If so, you may want to wait until you purchase your next one and title it in the name of your trust. Some states do allow you to name a beneficiary for your vehicle—if yours does, your trust should be the beneficiary. Ask your attorney how this works in your state, or call your state's license bureau. You may also want to check with your insurance company to make sure your coverage will stay in effect if you change the title or if you need to make any changes with them.

Sole Proprietorship

Your business licenses and DBA (doing business as) should be changed to show your living trust as the owner.

Solely-Owned Corporation

The appropriate corporate records will need to be prepared to transfer title and share certificates will need to be re-registered in the name of your trust.

Partnership/Corporation Interests

If you are involved in any real estate or other partnerships or corporations, your interest should be assigned to your trust. This probably will not disturb the existing agreement or affect your partners in any way, but you should check the partnership agreement or corporate by-laws just to be sure. Your attorney can help you if you need assistance.

Part Five

ADDITIONAL TAX PLANNING WITH IRREVOCABLE OPTIONS

Part Five— ADDITIONAL TAX PLANNING WITH IRREVOCABLE OPTIONS

PLANNING BEYOND YOUR LIVING TRUST

You may need additional tax planning beyond your A-B or A-B-C living trust as explained in Part Three. If so, you may be interested in one or more of the options in this section.

Keep in mind that these are *in addition to* your living trust. *None* of these will replace your living trust. Your living trust is the foundation for *all* of your estate planning needs.

Notice, too, that these are *irrevocable*. Up until now, we have been discussing a living trust which is *revocable*—remember, it can be changed or cancelled at any time as your needs change. An irrevocable trust, on the other hand, cannot be changed or cancelled once the final document has been signed. If you decide to use one of these in your tax planning, make sure you read the document very carefully and that you completely understand it before you sign anything. You'll also want to have the documents prepared by an estate planning attorney who has experience in this area.

THE IRREVOCABLE LIFE INSURANCE TRUST

Most people own some amount of life insurance and there are very good reasons for doing so at all ages. When you are young, life insurance can provide for your family in the event you die prematurely. Life insurance can also be very valuable later in life—to provide income for your family, to provide funds to buy out a business, or to pay estate taxes.

The trust owns your insurance for you

However, many people don't realize that these life insurance proceeds, while not subject to probate proceedings (unless, for some reason, you name your *estate* as the beneficiary), are included in your estate when determining *estate taxes*. Depending on the amount of insurance you have, this can dramatically increase the value of your estate—and the amount of estate taxes that must be paid.

An irrevocable life insurance trust lets your beneficiaries benefit from the insurance proceeds *and* keeps the value of the insurance out of your taxable estate, potentially saving your family thousands of dollars in estate taxes. How? Very simply, the life insurance trust owns your insurance policy *for* you. And since you don't personally own the insurance, it won't be included in your taxable estate when you die. (Sound familiar? The concept is basically the same as a living trust and how it avoids probate.)

Who Can Benefit From An Irrevocable Life Insurance Trust

If you are single and your net estate—including your life insurance—is more than $600,000, or if you are married and your total estate is over $1.2 million, an irrevocable life insurance trust is something you should seriously consider. If your estate is less than this, it is exempt from estate taxes so it doesn't matter if you are the owner of the policies. You just need to name your living trust as the beneficiary of your insurance as we explained earlier.

Let's look at a couple of examples:

Let's say you are single and, after subtracting out loans and debts, your net worth is $600,000 in "regular" assets (real estate, stocks, etc.) plus you have $200,000 in life insurance. The value of your estate would be $800,000 and when you die, $75,000 will be due in estate taxes. (Remember, the rate *starts* at 37% for each dollar over $600,000—and it goes up from there.)

On the other hand, if you have an irrevocable life insurance trust, the trust (not you) would own the insurance, so it would not be included as part of your estate. Your taxable estate, then, would only be $600,000, equal to the $600,000 exemption you are allowed. The life insurance trust just saved you $75,000 in estate taxes, leaving that much more for your beneficiaries.

Single Person's Estate

Without Life Insurance Trust		With Life Insurance Trust	
$ 600,000	Net worth (assets less debts)	$ 600,000	Net worth (assets less debts)
+ 200,000	Life insurance you own	+ 00	Life insurance you own
$ 800,000	Net estate	$ 600,000	Net estate
- 75,000	Federal estate taxes*	- 00	Federal estate taxes*
$ 725,000	Balance	$ 600,000	Balance
+ 00	Proceeds from insurance trust	+ 200,000	Proceeds from insurance trust
$ 725,000	*In assets for your beneficiaries*	*$ 800,000*	*In assets for your beneficiaries*

* After using $600,000 estate tax exemption.

Here's another example. Let's say you are married and your net estate is $1.6 million, $400,000 of which is in life insurance. With an A-B living trust, remember, you can protect $1.2 million from estate taxes. The remaining $400,000 will be subject to estate taxes of approximately $153,000. However, if you have an irrevocable life insurance trust, this $400,000 will not be included in your estate—and that means about $153,000 more for your beneficiaries.

Married Couple's Estate

Without Life Insurance Trust		With Life Insurance Trust	
$1,200,000	Net worth (assets less debts)	$1,200,000	Net worth (assets less debts)
+ 400,000	Life insurance you own	+ 00	Life insurance you own
$1,600,000	Net estate	$1,200,000	Net estate
- 153,000	Federal estate taxes*	- 00	Federal estate taxes*
$1,447,000	Balance	$1,200,000	Balance
+ 00	Proceeds from insurance trust	+ 400,000	Proceeds from insurance trust
$1,447,000	*In assets for your beneficiaries*	*$1,600,000*	*In assets for your beneficiaries*

* Taxes with an A-B living trust. Otherwise, you would pay an additional $255,000 in estate taxes.

Which Life Insurance Is Included In Your Taxable Estate

Your taxable estate will include all life insurance proceeds for which you have any "incidents of ownership" as defined by the IRS. Basically, you would have an incident of ownership if you pay premiums or control any use of the policy, such as being able to change the beneficiary(ies), cancel the policy, borrow against it, assign it or revoke an assignment, pledge the policy for a loan, or have a reversionary interest of more than 5% of the value of the policy immediately before your death (meaning you, not your named beneficiary, retain control over who will receive the proceeds if your beneficiary dies before you).

For example, your employer may provide life insurance as a benefit. You don't own the policy (your employer does), but you can name the beneficiary and change it at any time. The amount of this insurance, then, would be included in your taxable estate when you die. "Death benefits" from a fraternal organization or lodge would also be included.

Giving Ownership Of Your Insurance To Someone Else Is Risky

You could give away the ownership of your insurance to someone else—this *would* keep the insurance out of your taxable estate without setting up a life insurance trust. But this can also be risky.

Let's say you make your spouse owner of your insurance. You can't be sure which of you will outlive the other, and if your spouse dies first, the cash (or termination) value of the policy would be included in your spouse's taxable estate. Also, ownership of the insurance would revert to you. So that doesn't help much. There may also be a gift tax involved. And if you die within three years of changing the ownership, the transfer will be considered invalid by the IRS and the insurance will become part of your taxable estate.

But, perhaps more importantly, when you give someone else ownership of your insurance, you are giving up all control over the policy. The new owner can change the beneficiary(ies), take the cash value, even cancel the policy and leave you with no insurance. You may think you can trust this person now, but there could be some problems later if you were to have a major disagreement or, in the case of your spouse, if you divorce.

Setting up an irrevocable life insurance trust is a much safer alternative. It will let you make sure the proceeds are distributed the way you want and avoid estate taxes by removing all incidents of ownership.

You can name anyone you want as beneficiary of your trust

How An Irrevocable Life Insurance Trust Works

When you set up the trust, you will name a trustee to manage the trust for you. Following the instructions in your trust, the trustee will purchase a life insurance policy with you as the insured and the trust as the owner of the policy. In most cases, the trust will also be the beneficiary of the policy. So when the insurance benefit is paid after your death, the trustee will collect the funds and distribute them as you have instructed to your beneficiaries—without probate, income taxes or estate taxes.

Why The Trust Should Be Beneficiary Of The Insurance Policy

If you name your trust as beneficiary, the insurance company will pay the proceeds to the trust and your trustee can then use the funds according to the instructions you put in your trust. For example, your trustee could purchase assets from your living trust, replacing hard assets with cash to pay income and estate taxes, preventing a distress sale of the assets.

Also, if one of your beneficiaries is incompetent when you die, your trustee can invest that beneficiary's share and provide for his/her care for as long as needed. If you had named this person as a beneficiary of the life insurance policy, the insurance company probably would not pay to him/her direct, insisting instead on court supervision through a conservatorship.

Beneficiaries Of Your Life Insurance Trust

Just like your living trust, you can name anyone you want as beneficiaries of your insurance trust, and you can put any restrictions you want on the distributions. For example, you may want to provide for your children's or grandchildren's educations, then distribute the remaining proceeds among all your beneficiaries. You may also want to provide your estate with cash to pay estate taxes.

Funding Your Insurance Trust

Where does the trustee get the money to purchase the insurance? From you, but in a special way. If you give the money direct to the trustee, it could be subject to a gift tax. You also want to make sure you avoid any incidents of ownership in the policy to keep it out of your estate. So here's what you can do.

You may already know that each year you can give away up to $10,000 to an individual or organization with no gift tax. (If you are married, you and your spouse together can give up to $20,000.) That means you can give up to $10,000 each year ($20,000 if married) to each beneficiary of your insurance trust. But instead of making the gift directly to the beneficiaries, you give it to the trustee of your trust. The trustee then notifies each trust beneficiary that a gift has been received on his/her behalf and, unless he/she elects to receive the gift now, the trustee will invest the funds—by paying the premium on the insurance policy.

This is called a *demand right* because your beneficiaries are sent a written notice giving them the opportunity to demand the gift. When they decline, they forfeit this right. (The notification is also called a *Crummey letter*, because the procedure was proved valid in a case brought by a Mr. Crummey.) Of course, for this to work, your beneficiaries need to be informed and understand *not* to take the gift now, waiting instead for the insurance proceeds. By using this approach, you can make sure you have no incidents of ownership in the policy.

If you want to gift the full $10,000 annually (or $20,000 by husband and wife) per beneficiary, your trust will need to include an additional provision. That's because if a beneficiary of your insurance trust refuses a gift from you that exceeds $5,000 or 5% of his/her individual share of the trust, *the excess is considered to be a gift by that beneficiary to the other beneficiaries*. This gift does *not* qualify for the $10,000 gift tax exclusion, so your beneficiaries would have a gift tax liability.

To solve this problem, your insurance trust can be divided into separate shares, one for each of your beneficiaries, with the trust assets (the insurance policy) allocated among the shares. Then, when a beneficiary refuses a gift from you that exceeds this *5 & 5 limitation*, the beneficiary is making a gift of the excess to himself/herself—not to the other beneficiaries. This eliminates any gift tax liability.

Transferring Existing Policies Into Your Trust

Having the trustee purchase new insurance on your life is the best way to fund your trust and make sure you have no incidents of ownership in the policy. But you can transfer existing policies into your trust, although it is somewhat more complicated and risky. That's because of the "three year rule" we mentioned

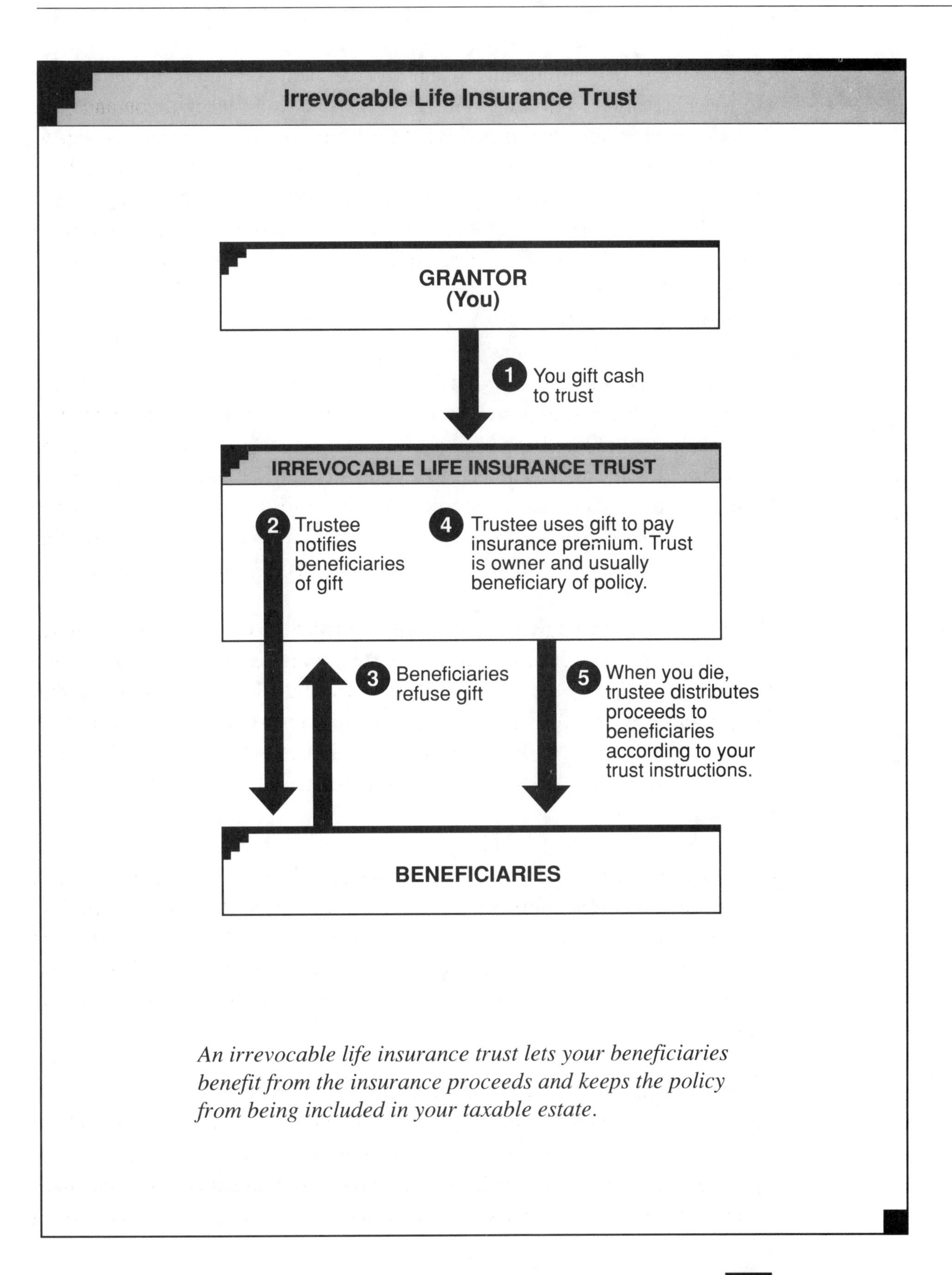

An irrevocable life insurance trust lets your beneficiaries benefit from the insurance proceeds and keeps the policy from being included in your taxable estate.

earlier—if you die within three years of transferring the policy into the trust, the transfer is considered invalid by the IRS, and the insurance would be included in your taxable estate. Also, depending on the replacement value of your existing policies (what it would cost to buy them now), you probably would have to pay a gift tax. If you want to transfer existing policies to your trust, you should talk with an insurance professional.

Selecting A Trustee

To get the tax benefits, you cannot be the trustee of your insurance trust. So you will need to name someone else as your trustee. Many people choose corporate trustees because of their experience—they will ensure the trust is correctly administered and the premiums paid.

Even though you can't be the trustee, you still have some control over your trust. The trustee you select must follow the instructions you put in your trust. And, remember, your trust owns the insurance policy—that is very different from giving the ownership away to another person.

When You Should Set Up An Irrevocable Life Insurance Trust

You can set one up at any time, but because the trust must be irrevocable, some people wait until they are in their 50's or 60's. By that time, family relationships have pretty much settled—and you know who you want to include (and exclude) as a beneficiary. Just make sure you don't wait too long—you could become uninsurable.

Seek Professional Assistance

If you think an irrevocable life insurance trust would be of value to you and your family, you may want to talk with a qualified insurance agent, estate planning attorney, or financial advisor who has worked with these trusts. Make sure the document is prepared by an estate planning attorney who has experience in preparing irrevocable life insurance trusts.

And, don't forget, this is an *irrevocable* trust. Once you've signed the trust, you can't make any changes. Read the document carefully and make sure it is exactly what you want *before* you sign.

THE CHARITABLE REMAINDER TRUST

There are many advantages to doing charitable planning now—you can secure a lifetime income, save on income and estate taxes, enjoy the satisfaction of making the gift and, if you wish, receive public recognition. And because the organization knows it will receive the gift at some point in the future, it can plan future projects and programs now—and benefit even before it receives the gift.

One of the most commonly used forms of charitable tax planning is called the charitable remainder trust. It is a way you can convert a highly appreciated asset (such as real estate or stocks) into a lifetime income *without* having to pay capital gains taxes on the sale *or* estate taxes upon your death. At the same time, you can benefit one or more charities or organizations that have special meaning to you.

Who Can Benefit From A Charitable Remainder Trust

Generally, if you are age 50 or older, own a highly appreciated asset, are in a high income bracket, would like to enjoy your profits now but want to avoid capital gains and estate taxes, and if charitable giving appeals to you, you can probably benefit from a charitable remainder trust.

How A Charitable Remainder Trust Works

You place the highly appreciated asset into an irrevocable trust, naming one or more qualified charities as beneficiary. The trustee then sells the asset at full market value, paying no taxes on the capital gain, and re-invests the proceeds in income-producing assets, which will grow tax-free. For the rest of your life, the trust will pay you an income. When you die, the *remainder* of the trust assets (the principal) will go to the charity.

If You Sell The Property Yourself

Of course, you could just sell the property yourself and reinvest the proceeds, but you would pay more in income and estate taxes and have less left for your beneficiaries. Let's look at an example.

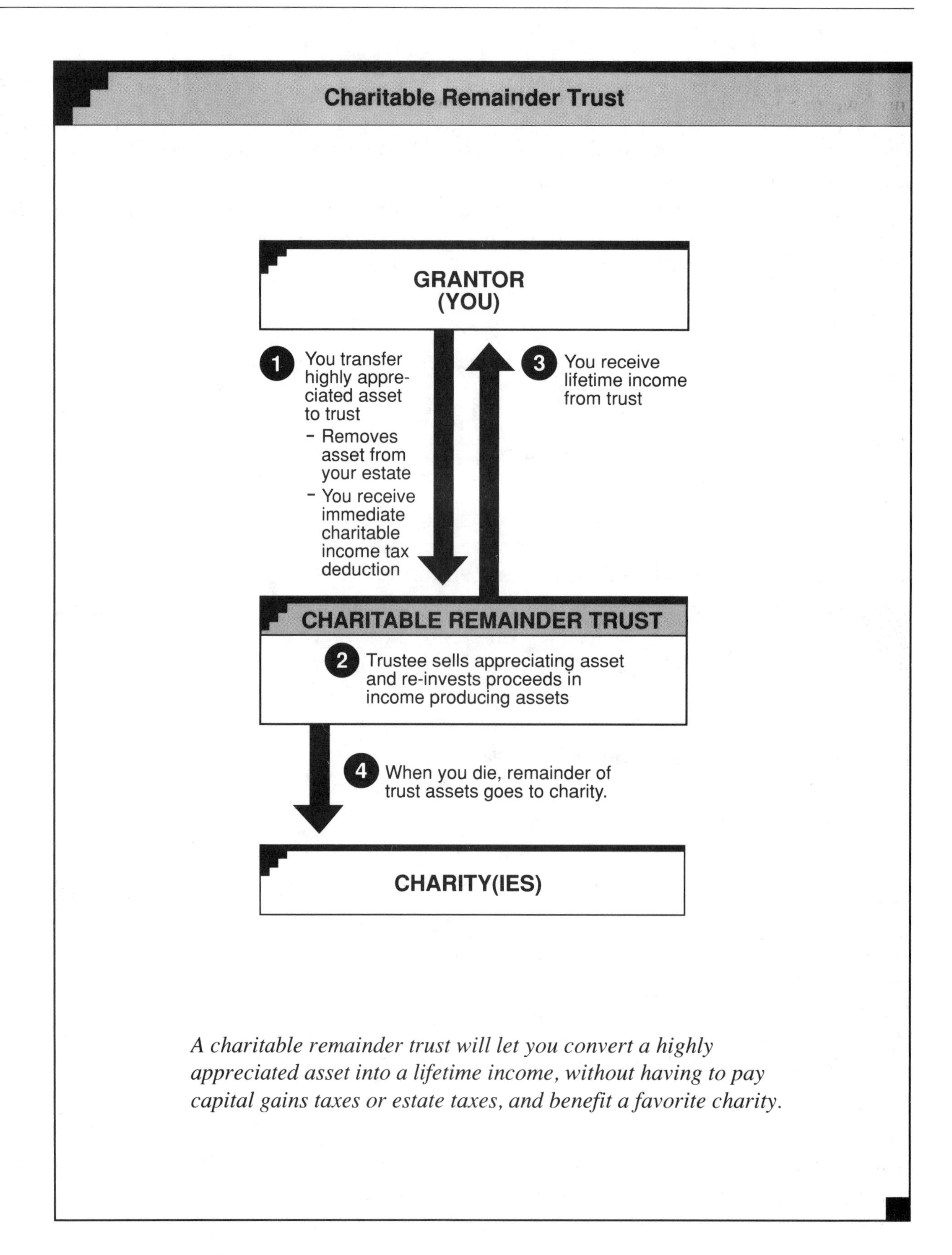

A charitable remainder trust will let you convert a highly appreciated asset into a lifetime income, without having to pay capital gains taxes or estate taxes, and benefit a favorite charity.

Convert a highly appreciated asset into lifetime income

Let's say 20 years ago you bought a piece of real estate for $100,000 that is now worth $500,000—a nice investment. But now, say at age 55, you would rather have the money so you can relax and not have to worry about it anymore.

If you sell the property, you would have a capital gain of $400,000, which is taxable as ordinary income in the year you sell—so you would have to pay approximately $113,000 in federal income taxes. That leaves you with only $387,000 to re-invest.

When you die, estate taxes will also have to be paid. Let's say that your entire estate at that time is $1,400,000. This would put you in a 40% estate tax bracket (remember that estate taxes *start* at 37% on every dollar over $600,000 and go up from there). So you would lose another $154,800 from the property in estate taxes. That makes a total of $267,800 in income and estate taxes—leaving only $232,200 of the original $500,000 for your beneficiaries.

Without A Charitable Remainder Trust	
Current market value	$ 500,000
Federal income taxes on $400,000 gain	- 113,000
Balance to re-invest	$ 387,000
Estate taxes (40%)	- 154,800
Left for beneficiaries	$ 232,200

If You Use A Charitable Remainder Trust

With a charitable remainder trust, you eliminate the income taxes on the capital gain *and* estate taxes. Plus, in the year you place the property into the trust, you can take an immediate charitable income tax deduction, reducing your current income taxes. The trustee sells the property for the full market value and, because there are no capital gains taxes on the sale, re-invests the full $500,000 in a balanced portfolio (like stocks and bonds) to provide you with a lifetime taxable income. Now the entire $500,000 is working for you, instead of only $387,000. (In just a moment, we'll show you how you can replace the full value of this property for your own beneficiaries.)

Eliminate capital gains and estate taxes on the asset

How Much Income You Receive

How much income you receive from the trust is flexible, and will depend upon how much income you need, the value of the property, your age, life expectancy, etc. Let's say you elect to receive an annual income from the trust equal to 8% of the trust's assets. For the first year, then, you would receive $40,000 in income (8% of $500,000). If the trust is well managed, it will grow quickly. That's because whatever the trustee earns over your 8% will be added to the trust assets and re-invested *tax-free*.

The trust is re-valued each year to determine the dollar amount of income you will receive, so as the trust grows your income will too (you'll be getting 8% of a larger number). Your trust can include a "make-up" provision, so if the trust doesn't earn enough to pay you the 8% one year, it will make up the difference to you in a better year. By the way, since you have elected to receive a *percentage* of the value of the trust assets, this would be called a "charitable remainder *unitrust*."

You can elect instead to receive a *fixed* amount of income each year. In this case, the trust would be called a "charitable remainder *annuity* trust." This means the amount of income you receive is guaranteed—it will not go down if the trust has an "off" investment year, but it also will not increase if the trust does well. Because they want protection against inflation, many people prefer to receive a percentage of the trust assets as income (the unitrust).

Determining The Income Tax Deduction

The charitable income tax deduction is based on the amount of income you receive, the size of your gift, and your age. (Basically, the more you elect to receive in income, the less your deduction will be.) It is limited to either 30% or 50% of your adjusted gross income—depending on how the IRS defines the charity and the type of asset involved. If you don't use the entire deduction the first year, you can carry it forward for up to five additional years.

Types Of Assets Suitable For A Charitable Remainder Trust

The best assets for a charitable remainder trust are those that have greatly appreciated in value since you purchased them, including real estate, a closely-held company and publicly traded securities. Highly leveraged properties usually won't qualify (although you might consider paying off the loan).

Selecting A Trustee

Although you can be trustee of your charitable remainder trust, it's usually not a good idea because you can lose the tax advantages if the trust is not administered correctly. You can name anyone you want but, because of the investment and administrative experience required, many people choose a corporate trustee. Some charities also like to be the trustee, and frequently the charity will pay for the cost of setting up the trust in return for being named the trustee in addition to beneficiary. Keep in mind that, if you elect to receive a percentage of the trust's value (the unitrust), you are depending on the trustee's investment performance for your income. So you will want to make sure the trustee has a good past performance record as an investor.

Even though you probably won't be your own trustee, you still have some control. Until you die, your *trust* controls the assets you transfer to the trust—not the charity that will eventually receive them. And the trustee you select must follow the instructions you put in your trust. Also, you can retain the right to change the trustee at any time. You may also be able to change the beneficiary of the trust—but only to another qualified charity. Otherwise, you will lose the tax advantages. But, generally, once an irrevocable trust is signed, you cannot make any other changes. So you will want to be sure you read the document carefully and make sure it is exactly what you want *before* you sign.

Who Can Receive Income From The Trust

In our example, the trust was set up to pay a lifetime income to you, but there is quite a bit of flexibility here. If you are married, the trust can pay an income for as long as *either* of you lives. Your trust could also be set up to last for the combined lives of your children. For that matter, the person who receives the income doesn't even have to be related to you—or even be a person. And instead of lasting for someone's lifetime, the trust can be set up to last for a set number of years—up to 20.

You can also defer the income until later. For example, you may want to sell your property now to be free from management headaches, but you aren't yet ready to retire and don't need the income. You can go ahead and set up the trust, taking the income tax deduction in that year, and the trustee will invest the trust assets. By the time you are ready to receive an income, the trust, with good management, will be substantially greater in value—resulting in a higher income for you.

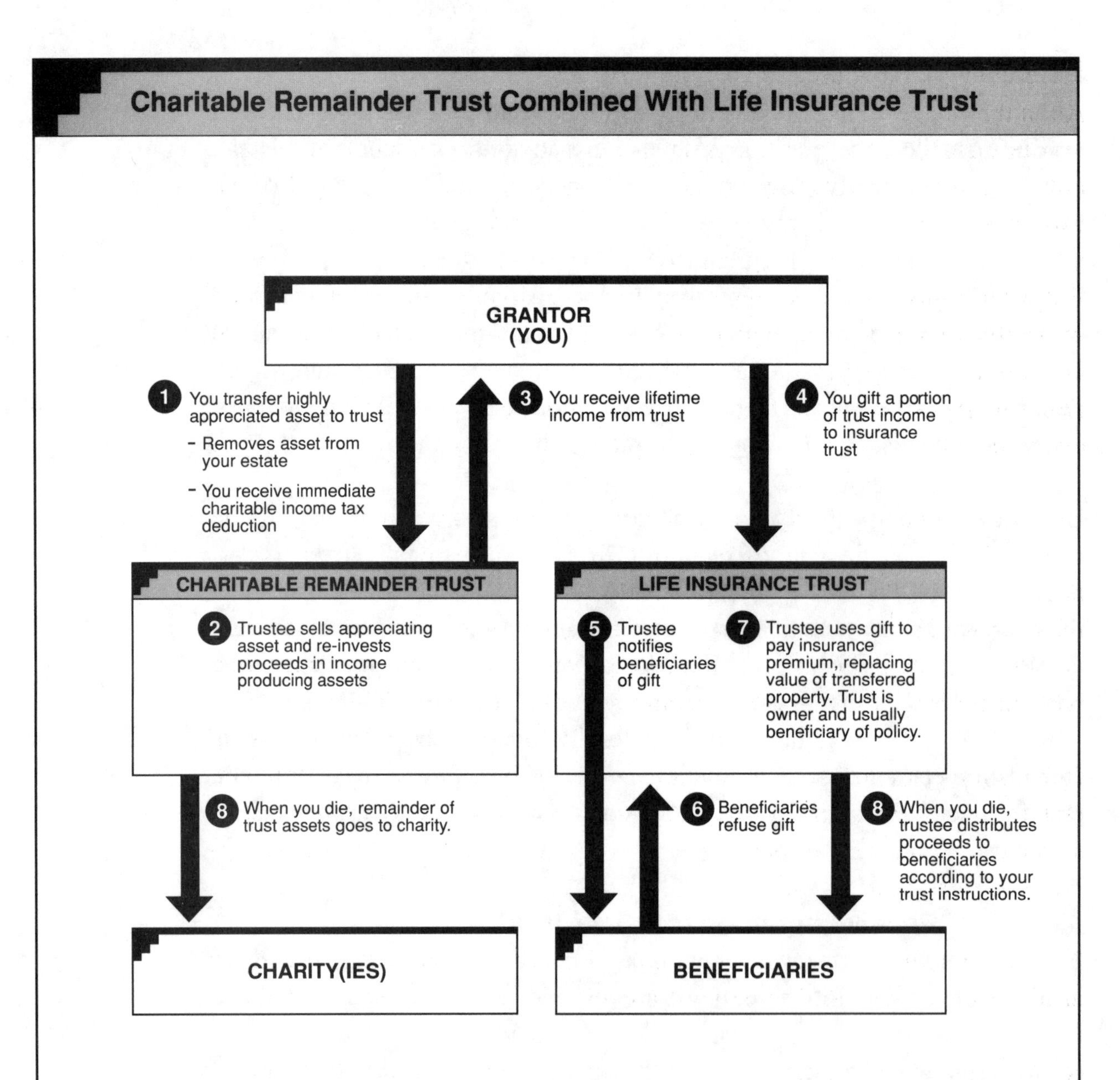

By using the income tax savings and part of the income you receive from the charitable remainder trust, you can fund an irrevocable life insurance trust to replace the value of the asset that has been placed in the charitable remainder trust.

Replacing The Asset

All of this sounds great, you may say, if you have no children. Or your estate may be sizeable—the property you place in a charitable remainder trust may only be a small percentage of your assets, so your children may be well taken care of.

But what if this asset makes up a good portion of your estate? Your children probably wouldn't be too happy about losing out on such a large inheritance and, quite honestly, you probably wouldn't feel very good about that either. Don't worry—there is a very easy way to replace the value of the asset so everyone wins.

By using the income tax savings and part of the income you receive from the charitable remainder trust, you can fund an irrevocable life insurance trust. Each year you can "gift" money to the life insurance trust, and the trustee can then purchase enough life insurance to replace the value of the property. When you die, your children will receive the full proceeds from the insurance trust without probate, and free from income and estate taxes.

Life insurance is the fastest and most inexpensive way to replace the property. But if you are uninsurable, the trustee can buy other appreciating assets—such as zero-coupon bonds, stocks or real estate—to replace the value of the property you transfer to the trust.

This combination of the charitable remainder trust and irrevocable life insurance trust is a "win-win" situation for everyone:

- You can take an immediate charitable income tax deduction and remove a highly appreciated asset from your estate—saving income and estate taxes.
- You receive a guaranteed lifetime income without the headaches or uncertainty of having to manage the investment.
- When you die, your children (or other beneficiaries) receive cash from the life insurance trust, replacing the value of the asset—income tax, estate tax and probate free.
- And you are able to make a substantial gift to one or several charities.

THE CHARITABLE LEAD TRUST

Basically, a charitable lead trust is just the opposite of a charitable remainder trust. With a charitable lead trust, the charity receives the income from the trust now and your beneficiaries will eventually receive the principal.

A charitable lead trust can also reduce your income taxes, reduce or eliminate your estate taxes, and allow you to make a contribution to one or more qualified charities. Unlike a remainder trust, however, you would be interested in a lead trust if you currently do not need the income and want a beneficiary other than the charity (usually your spouse and/or children) to eventually receive the trust assets.

If the annual income paid to the charity is a percentage, and the amount fluctuates depending on investment performance, it's called a charitable lead *unitrust*. If the income is a fixed amount (the same dollar amount paid every year), it's called a charitable lead *annuity* trust.

ADDITIONAL TAX PLANNING THROUGH CHARITABLE GIVING

Here are some other forms of charitable giving which also provide tax benefits and may appeal to you.

Pooled Income Fund

You may be interested in a pooled income fund if you don't have sufficient assets to contribute to a charitable remainder or lead trust, or if you would prefer to make smaller contributions over a period of time. You make these contributions directly to the charity, and the charity will "pool" your contributions with others and invest them together. Your contributions then become "shares" of the fund (similar to a mutual fund). You (or a designated beneficiary) will receive a lifetime income from the fund. When the last beneficiary dies, your shares will transfer to the charity. Your gifts can be made in cash, stocks, or bonds, and you receive an income tax deduction in each year you make a contribution.

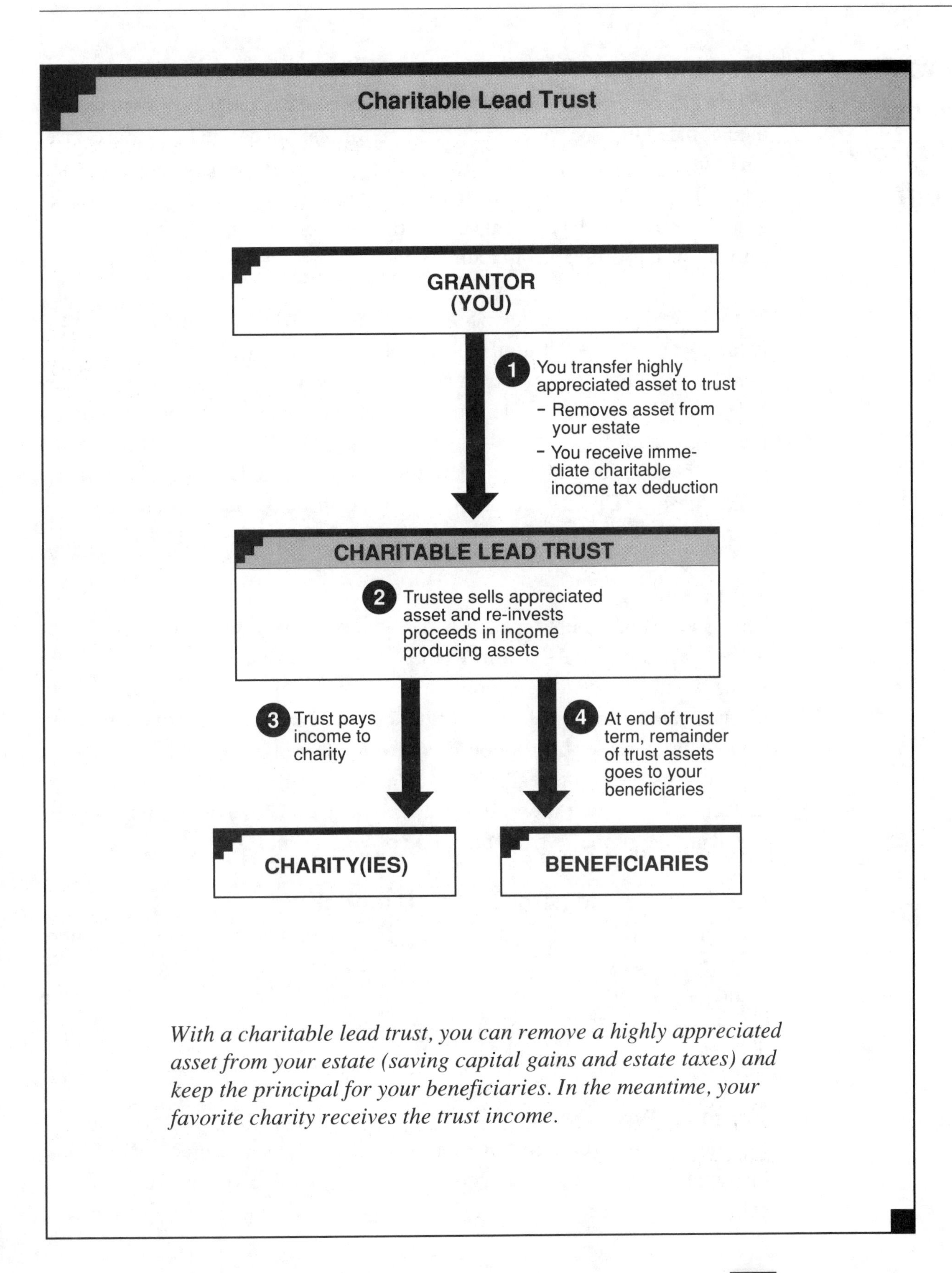

With a charitable lead trust, you can remove a highly appreciated asset from your estate (saving capital gains and estate taxes) and keep the principal for your beneficiaries. In the meantime, your favorite charity receives the trust income.

Both you and the charity can benefit from your gift

Gift Annuity

With a gift annuity, you (or whoever you name as the beneficiary) will receive a guaranteed income for life in exchange for making a direct gift to a charity (in cash, real estate or another asset). The income will be paid in the form of an annuity, which means each payment you receive will be for the same dollar amount. Part of each payment is a return to you of your gift (the principal), so only a portion is taxable as ordinary income.

You can begin receiving the income immediately when the gift is made or the income can be delayed until a later date (usually at retirement, when your income—and tax bracket—is lower). If the income is delayed, this is called a *deferred* gift annuity. Under this option, the income will be higher because the original investment will have time to grow. Regardless of when the income begins, you can take a charitable income tax deduction in the year you make the gift. Upon your death (or the death of the last beneficiary), the charity will keep the remaining principal and any undistributed income.

Life Estate

This is an arrangement through which you can give a portion or all of your home, vacation home or farm to the charity of your choice while you are living. Until your death, you continue to enjoy the property as if you still own it—you can live on it, take care of it, and keep any income it may generate. You would consider this option if you were planning to give the property to the charity after your death, but wanted to take the charitable income tax deduction while you are still alive. You will also save on estate taxes by removing the property from the value of your estate.

Conservation, Mineral And/Or Use Rights

You can give a charity the right to *use* a piece of property for a certain number of years as a public park, a wildlife refuge, an historic landmark, etc. Or you could give away just the mineral rights to a piece of real estate and keep the land in your family. The tax advantages of this type of gift are generally less than others we've mentioned.

Personal Property

You may have certain investments or valuables (for example, art, musical instruments, books, etc.) that you want to give to a charity—not to have them sold and the proceeds re-invested, but rather to have them be enjoyed as you have enjoyed them. For you to receive a charitable income tax deduction, the gift must be related to the charity's tax-exempt purpose—for example, giving artwork, antiques or jewelry to a museum, books to a university or library, musical instruments to a symphony, etc.

Insurance

This is an often overlooked gift. You can give an old policy to a charity, making it both the owner and the beneficiary. Or you can work with a charity and have it purchase a new policy on your life (the charity should be the applicant, owner and beneficiary). In either case, you can receive a charitable income tax deduction.

Qualifying The Charity

You will want to make sure the organization meets IRS guidelines as a "qualified" charity—otherwise you could end up losing the tax advantages. The IRS publishes a list of qualified charities and their tax status, which determines whether a 30% or 50% income tax deduction will apply. The charity will also have a *determination letter* from the IRS which verifies its tax status.

You may also want to research the organization before finalizing your gift. One source of information is the *National Charities Information Bureau*, which evaluates many national not-for-profit organizations. Its published reports are available for a nominal charge. Call 212-929-6300 for more information.

Seek Professional Assistance

If you think charitable giving would be of value in your tax planning and would like more information, consult with your favorite charity, tax planning attorney, CPA, insurance specialist and/or a corporate trustee. It is also a good idea to discuss a potential gift with the organization while you are in the planning stages—they may be able to give you valuable insight and suggestions on how the gift can be most useful to them. They may also be able to recommend an experienced attorney to prepare the legal documents.

Remember, it is critical that the documents are prepared properly. Make sure you read and understand everything before you sign. You should also check to be sure the document contains the correct legal name and specific location (including address) of the organization you want to receive the gift.

GRANTOR RETAINED INCOME TRUST (GRIT)

There are advantages to transferring (gifting) assets to your children now while you are living, instead of waiting until you die—especially if the assets will continue to appreciate in value. Removing the assets from your taxable estate now, while the value is much lower than it will be at your death, can potentially save your estate thousands of dollars in estate taxes. And you have the satisfaction of seeing your children enjoy the gift.

By using a Grantor Retained Income Trust (GRIT), you can transfer these assets to your children without paying any estate or gift taxes, and you can leverage the current value of your gift into a much larger one.

How It Works

With a GRIT, you transfer one or more appreciating assets into an irrevocable trust for up to ten years. During this time (the *term* of the trust), you receive income from the trust. (That's where this trust gets its name—the grantor retains the income from the trust.) At the end of the trust term, the trust principal is distributed to your beneficiaries.

As long as you survive the term of the trust, the assets are removed from your taxable estate so estate taxes are eliminated. And because the gift is delayed, your gift tax liability is based on an amount *less* than the actual gift you are making. However, you probably won't actually *pay* any gift taxes (we'll explain this a little later). During the term of the trust, the trust assets grow tax-free and, with good management, by the end of the trust term your original gift will have grown significantly in value. So your children will receive an appreciated asset free from both estate taxes and gift taxes.

Here's An Example

Let's say you want to reduce your taxable estate and give your son $100,000. Rather than making an outright gift today, you place $100,000 in assets into a GRIT for ten years.

Because you have retained the right to receive all the income from the trust, and you pay income taxes when you receive it, the IRS assigns an *economic value* to this right and reduces the present value of the gift you make to the trust for gift tax purposes. The reduction is determined from tables published by the

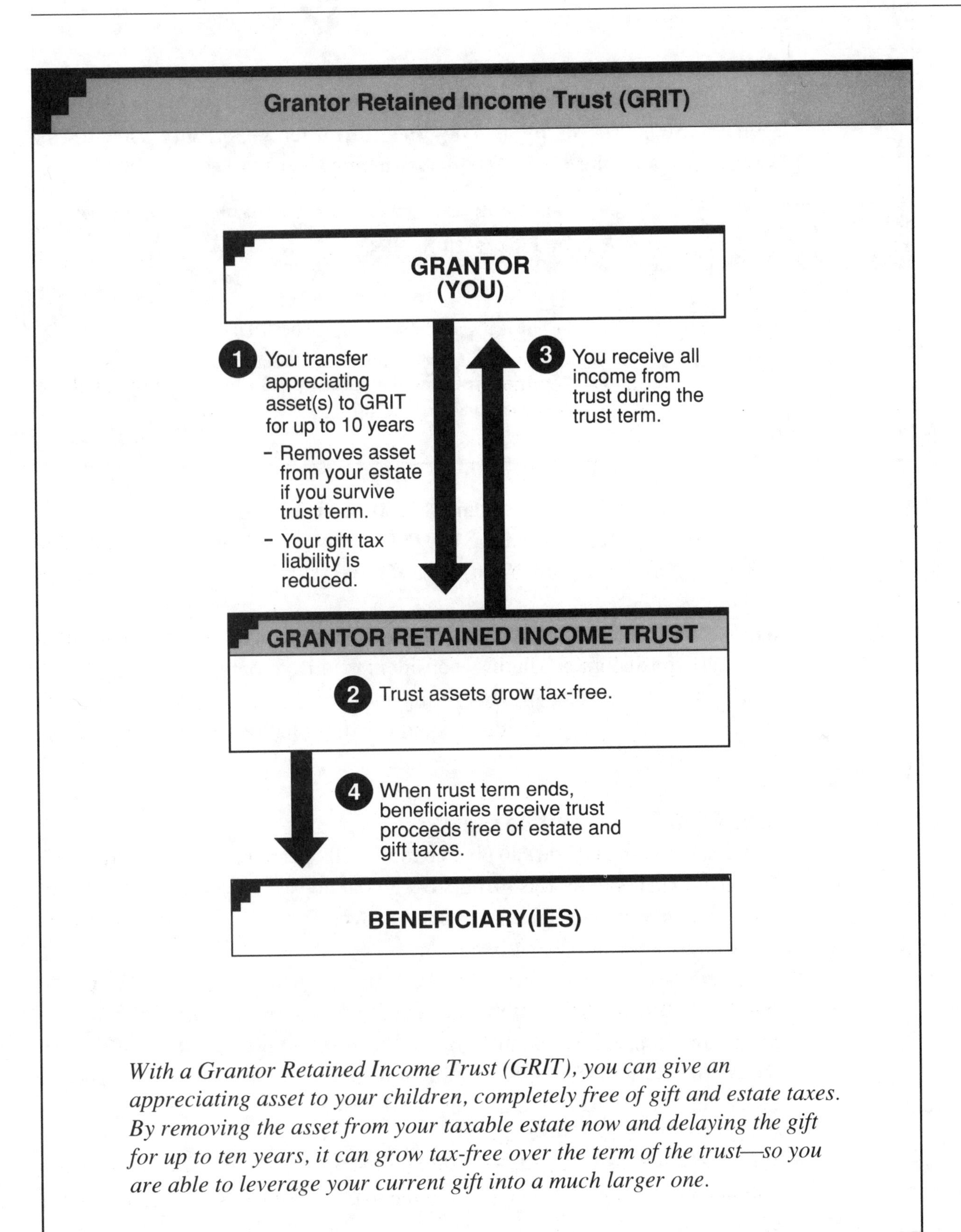

With a Grantor Retained Income Trust (GRIT), you can give an appreciating asset to your children, completely free of gift and estate taxes. By removing the asset from your taxable estate now and delaying the gift for up to ten years, it can grow tax-free over the term of the trust—so you are able to leverage your current gift into a much larger one.

IRS, the amount of the gift, current interest rates and the term of the trust. Assuming an interest rate of 9.6% on our example, this economic value is equal to $60,000—so, by delaying the gift for ten years, only $40,000 (the present value of the $100,000 gift) is subject to gift taxes.

Reduced Gift Tax Liability

$100,000	Original market value of assets placed in GRIT
- 60,000	Economic value of income you receive from the trust for the next ten years (as determined by IRS tables)
$ 40,000	Taxable present value of the gift

Here's another way to understand this. What would your son have to invest today at 9.6% interest to have $100,000 in ten years? $40,000—so $40,000 is the *present* value of the *future* gift of $100,000.

This is a very smart way to leverage your gift—and make the most out of what you can afford to give. The IRS considers the gift to be worth only $40,000, you're actually putting in $100,000—and, with good investment performance, by the time the gift is distributed it will probably be worth much more than $100,000.

Eliminating The Gift Tax

In general, of course, you can give up to $10,000 per person per year free from any gift tax. However, this gift tax exclusion doesn't apply to GRITs, so the gift tax is determined as we explained above.

But that doesn't mean you will pay a gift tax when you set up your GRIT. Instead, the present value of the gift is applied to your $600,000 federal estate tax exemption. (In our example, then, the $40,000 present value of the gift would reduce your $600,000 exemption to $560,000—which you can use later.) So, unless you have already used up your $600,000 exemption, you won't actually pay a gift tax.

Reduce your estate taxes by making the gift now

You can also avoid paying any gift taxes on the appreciation of the trust assets, as long as your GRIT meets these requirements:

- You, as the grantor, must receive income from the trust—so the assets in the trust must produce *some* income (although the trust doesn't have to produce as much as the interest rate factor used to determine the economic value of this income—9.6% in our example).
- The term of the trust cannot exceed ten years—unless your trust contains your personal residence, life insurance or some personal use property such as artwork (in these limited cases, the trust can last up to 15 years).
- You cannot be trustee, your spouse shouldn't (or the trust could be disqualified), and your children can only be trustee while you are living (which can be a problem if you die during the term of the trust). So this is an excellent time to use a corporate trustee.

As long as your trust follows these rules, the *value* of the gift for gift tax purposes is locked in at the $40,000 present value—regardless of how much the trust grows. So your $100,000 gift which may grow to $200,000, $300,000 or even more, is completely free from any additional gift taxes.

If your trust does *not* follow these rules, when the trust ends there will be a gift tax due on the difference between the appreciated value of the trust and the present value when the trust was created ($40,000 in our example). This, of course, would completely defeat the purpose of setting up the trust. You can see how critical it is that your trust is properly prepared and that you see an experienced tax-planning attorney for advice and assistance.

If You Die Before The Trust Term Is Over

If you die before the term of the trust ends, the value of the trust assets as of the date of your death will be included in your taxable estate. However, the trust doesn't have to end when you die—if any estate taxes are owed, the trust can pay them and continue to grow tax-free until the trust term ends. So your son would still benefit from the tax-free appreciation of the trust assets.

Retaining A Second Right

In addition to retaining the right to the *income* from the trust (which you must do for the trust to qualify), you can choose to retain a second right—that of having the GRIT *discontinue* if you die before the trust term is over. (This is called a right of reversion.) This, of course, means your son wouldn't receive anything from the trust—because there would be no trust—and the full value of the trust assets at that time would be part of your taxable estate. But there is an advantage that often makes this worth doing.

Just as the IRS places an economic value on your right to receive trust income, there is a value to this right as well, which further reduces the present value of the gift. Using our earlier example, if you are around age 50 when the trust is established and you retain this second right, the $40,000 present value of the gift would be further reduced to around $30,000. (The exact value of this right, too, is determined from IRS tables and is based on your age.)

Gift Tax Liability Further Reduced

$100,000	Original market value of assets placed in GRIT
- 60,000	Economic value of income you receive from the trust for the next ten years (as determined by IRS tables)
$ 40,000	Taxable present value of the gift

Usually, depending on your age and health, you will want to retain this second right to reduce the present value of the gift as much as possible. There is, however, a limit on the value of this second right—it can't exceed 25% of the value of the first right (to receive income). So, in our example, the value of the reversion right cannot exceed $15,000 (25% of $60,000).

Maximizing Your $600,000 Exemption

Here's another way to get the most out of your GRIT. Depending on the size of your estate and how much you want (and can afford) to give, it's worth playing with some numbers to maximize your $600,000 exemption.

You can have more than one GRIT at the same time

In our example, the $40,000 present value of the gift is 40% of the $100,000 placed in the trust. So, if you wanted to use up your entire $600,000 exemption (and had the assets available), you could gift up to $1.5 million tax-free (40% of $1.5 million is $600,000). Your spouse could also set up a trust and use his/her exemption. If the trust assets are managed well and double in value over the next ten years, you and your spouse would end up giving your beneficiaries *$6 million—completely free from gift and estate taxes.* You have removed $3 million from your taxable estate (saving the estate taxes)—and, by taking full advantage of both $600,000 exemptions, you didn't have to pay any gift taxes.

Now, if you retain the second right (right of reversion), you and your spouse could gift even more. Continuing our earlier example where the present value of the gift is reduced to $30,000, your gifts could increase to $1.8 million each (30% of $1.8 million is $600,000). That's a combined gift of $3.6 million which, if it doubles in value, would grow to $7.2 million. If it triples in value, which is possible with good investment management, it would grow to $10.8 million. So by giving $3.6 million now, in just ten years your beneficiaries could receive *$10.8 million*—again, *with no estate or gift taxes.*

Selecting The Term Of The Trust

You can see that, to get the full advantages of a GRIT, you need to survive the trust term. So you will want to choose a reasonable length of time for your trust to exist. For example, if you are 90 years old, chances are you won't survive a ten-year trust. On the other hand, if you are 50 or 60 and in good health, a ten-year term is probably a pretty safe choice.

Also, keep in mind the longer the term of the trust, the lower the present value of the gift. For example, if we change our original example to only a five year trust (instead of ten), the present value of the $100,000 gift increases to a little more than $63,000. In other words, your son would have to invest over $63,000 at 9.6% to have $100,000 in five years. So you'll usually want to have the trust last as long as possible in your situation.

By the way, you can have more than one GRIT in existence at the same time. If you stagger them (so that they have different termination dates) and distribute the assets among several GRITs, you minimize your risk of having "all your eggs in one basket." In other words, if you have one GRIT and die before the trust ends, everything you've put into the trust comes back into your taxable estate. But if you spread the gifts over several trusts with different termination dates, chances are pretty good that at least some of the gifts will escape estate taxes. This is certainly something to consider in your estate planning strategy.

Selecting The Best Interest Rate

High interest rates are great for a GRIT, which makes this kind of trust particularly attractive in inflationary times. That's because the higher the interest rate at the time the trust is established, the greater the value the IRS assigns to the income you receive from the trust—which lowers the present value of the gift.

For instance, if the interest rate in our earlier example is 11%, the present value drops from $40,000 to about $35,000. In other words, your son would only have to invest $35,000 at 11% to have $100,000 in ten years. So you would be using less of your $600,000 exemption—and if you want, you can further reduce your taxable estate by putting more into your GRIT and making a larger gift to your son, gift tax and estate tax free.

By the way, you can choose the interest rate from several months before and after the date your trust is established, and since the rate is locked in when your trust is set up, you'll want to be aware of interest rate fluctuations to get the highest possible rate.

Selecting The Trustee

As we mentioned earlier, you can't be trustee, your spouse shouldn't, and it's risky for your children to be. So your best choice is a corporate trustee. You can see how valuable good investment management is to produce the best results from your trust, so you will want to select a trustee with a solid investment performance track record. Investment performance, however, shouldn't be your only criteria. We suggest you refer to page 108 for suggestions on how to evaluate a corporate trustee.

Naming Appropriate Beneficiaries

You'll notice in our example the beneficiary is your son. We've purposely avoided grandchildren as beneficiaries—and perhaps you should, too. That's because if a grandchild is the beneficiary of a GRIT, in addition to the gift tax we've been discussing, there will be a *generation skipping transfer tax* on the

value of the gift at the *end* of the trust term—which would include any appreciation. This is a very expensive tax (as we'll explain next).

Is A GRIT Right For You?

Whether or not you can benefit from a GRIT will depend on several factors—including your age, your health and the size of your estate. The type of assets you gift should also be a consideration—remember, the trust assets must produce some income. And you'll want to use a little arithmetic to see if a GRIT is a good tax-planning option for you. Here's why.

With a GRIT, your children receive the asset as a gift instead of as an inheritance, and only a portion of the gift receives a stepped-up basis—the rest retains your original cost basis (what you paid for it). This means that, if your children later sell the asset, they will have to pay income taxes on the gain—the difference between what they receive when the asset is sold and the cost basis. For this reason, you may want to consider putting into your GRIT only property that has a high cost basis. (You may want to refer back to page 20 for an explanation of stepped-up basis.)

However, you'll want to run the numbers to see which way is better for your situation. Does it work out better to leave the asset in your estate and pay estate taxes on it (which start at 37%), so it can receive a full stepped-up basis at your death? Or are you better off to place the asset in a GRIT, let it appreciate for up to ten years, and have your children pay income taxes on the gain whenever they sell it?

If the asset is one your children will probably not sell—for example, stock in a family business or the family farm—then a GRIT may be an especially attractive option for you since there won't be any income taxes to worry about. However, there are some special rules that apply to family owned property—so you will want to ask your attorney about the asset(s) you are considering for a GRIT.

Seek Professional Assistance

As you can see, it is very important that your GRIT is prepared properly. If you think you may be interested in one, you should seek a qualified estate planning attorney who has experience with GRITs to advise you, work with you to structure your trust to meet your needs, and prepare the documents.

Remember to ask questions, read the documents carefully and make sure you understand everything before you sign the documents—because, like all irrevocable trusts, you can't change your mind once the documents have been signed.

Advantages Of A GRIT

- ***Reduces Estate Taxes***—When you transfer the assets to the irrevocable trust during your lifetime, these assets are removed from your taxable estate. So, as long as you survive the term of the trust, there will be no estate taxes on these assets when you die.

- ***Gift Is Reduced For Gift Tax Purposes***—Because you are retaining the income from the trust and delaying the gift, your gift tax liability is based on an amount *less* than the actual gift you are making. However, this reduced gift tax liability is applied to your $600,000 exemption, so you probably won't actually pay any gift taxes.

- ***Tax-Free Growth***—During the term of the trust, the trust assets grow tax-free. So, if they are invested wisely, by the time the assets are distributed to your beneficiaries, they will be worth much more than the original gift.

- ***Tax-Free Gift To Your Beneficiaries***—Your beneficiaries will receive the appreciated trust proceeds completely free from estate taxes and gift taxes.

GENERATION SKIPPING TRANSFER (GST) TAX

If you are planning to leave assets to your grandchildren, you should be aware of the Generation Skipping Transfer (GST) tax. This tax applies if the inheritance skips a generation—for example, if you omit your children as beneficiaries and leave the inheritance directly to your grandchildren and younger generations.

In the past, generation skipping trusts were common, especially among the wealthy. The grandfather would set up a trust that distributed only income from the trust (no principal) to his children. The trust principal would be

distributed later to his grandchildren and future generations. This allowed the trust to grow tax-free and appreciate in value. And it avoided the heavy taxation that would have occurred if each generation had been taxed on the full inheritance. You can see how this was used to build wealth for several generations.

Contact a qualified professional for advice

Eventually, of course, Uncle Sam decided he wanted his share of taxes, just as if each generation had received its inheritance and paid taxes on it. So, if you leave substantial assets to your grandchildren and future generations—bypassing your children's generation—these assets may be subject to the Generation Skipping Transfer tax.

The bad news is that this GST tax is a *very expensive* tax—a flat rate of 55%. And keep in mind that this tax is *in addition to* estate taxes, which can also be as high as 55%. So if, for example, $10 million of a $15 million estate was left directly to the grandchildren with no estate planning, $5.5 million would be paid in estate taxes and another $2,475,000 would be paid in GST taxes—leaving only $2,025,000 for the beneficiaries!

Now, the good news is that everyone has a $1 million exemption from this tax. So, you and your spouse together can leave up to $2 million to your grandchildren and future generations free of this generation skipping tax.

If you have considerable assets to leave to your beneficiaries, you will need to see an experienced estate planning attorney. He/she will be able to advise you and help you make the best use of your options to meet your objectives and your beneficiaries' individual needs.

SUMMARY

We hope this section has been interesting and enlightening for you. For more information, make sure you contact a qualified professional. And remember that these are ways you can do tax planning *in addition to* your living trust—*they do not replace your living trust*, which provides the base for all of your estate planning needs.

Part Six

COMMONLY ASKED QUESTIONS

Part Six—
COMMONLY ASKED QUESTIONS

How Much Should I Own Before It's Worth It For Me To Have A Living Trust?

It's really not a matter of how much you own. Whether you are married or single, old or young, or have a modest or substantial estate—just about everyone can benefit from a living trust.

As we've explained in this book, a living trust does eliminate all probate costs and, depending on the size of your estate, it can also reduce or eliminate estate taxes. So, the larger your estate, the more money a living trust can save your family. On the other hand, a smaller estate will usually lose a greater percentage of its value to probate costs. And don't forget all the other problems that go with probate regardless of the size of your estate—it's slow, your family has no privacy or control, and a will can easily be contested.

But many people are just as interested in protecting themselves against probate while they are still alive. Remember, becoming physically or mentally incapacitated and losing control of their lives is a real concern of millions of older Americans—and those who will care for them. Having a living trust prevents a court conservatorship if this happens. And that's usually reason enough for many people to have a living trust—regardless of the size of their estate.

Don't forget, if you have minor children, a living trust also will prevent a court guardianship if something happens to you.

Probate Fees In My State Are Negotiable. Why Should I Have A Living Trust When Probate May Not Cost That Much?

In some states you can negotiate probate fees with your attorney, but be careful. "Negotiated" means an attorney can charge "whatever the market will bear," so you may end up paying more than if the fees were statutory (where the attorney's minimum fees are set by law). Also, you may find an attorney who will work for a lower fee but, remember, you usually get what you pay for—a more experienced attorney will probably be more expensive. In any case, don't forget that the costs of probate are much more than just financial.

Isn't A Living Trust Expensive?

A living trust does cost more to set up initially than a will does. But, remember that the cost of a will actually includes the costs of probate. A living trust, on the other hand, avoids all probate—and that can save your family many thousands of dollars. So when you put it all into perspective, a living trust is really quite a bargain.

I've Seen Several "Do-It-Yourself" Books And Kits. Can't I Do This Myself?

In order to be mass marketed, these kits and books must be pretty generic—so they can't begin to address every family's unique needs. As a result, they can be very dangerous. Planning your estate is not the time to compromise on quality just because you want to try and save a few dollars—remember, this is *your family* we're talking about. Besides, with so many attorneys doing living trusts now, you can probably get yours done at a very reasonable price. Instead of trying to do this yourself, you're much better off to first become educated about living trusts and then have a competent attorney do the legal documents for you. Then you'll be able to sleep at night, knowing your living trust has been done right.

By reading this book and completing our Personal and Financial Organizer ahead of time, you'll be an informed consumer. You'll understand the basics about living trusts, have a good idea of what you want your plan to be, and you'll be better prepared to ask appropriate questions. (Being informed and organized will also save you time and money.)

An experienced estate planning attorney can provide valuable guidance and assistance for your situation and assure that the documents are prepared correctly. It is very important, however, that you find the *right* attorney—preferably one who specializes in living trusts.

How Do I Find A Qualified Attorney To Do My Trust?

The best way, of course, is through a personal referral—ask someone who has a living trust. Or ask your friends, banker, trust officer, insurance agent, accountant, investment broker, financial advisor, family or business attorney, church/synagogue, or charity if they can recommend a qualified estate planning attorney who does living trusts. Then follow the guidelines we have provided on page 124. And don't forget to trust your instincts—it's very important for you to feel comfortable with the person doing your trust.

Are All Living Trust Documents The Same?

No. Although, in concept, all living trusts generally work the same way and contain the same basic provisions, the actual trust documents will vary from attorney to attorney. Although there are standardized trust forms, many attorneys use these as a starting point to write their own. Your trust document may also require some additional customization. That's why it's important to find an attorney who has experience in doing living trusts.

Do I Have To Stay With The Attorney Who Does My Trust?

No. While that attorney may like to have additional business from you, you're under no obligation to see him/her again. If you need any changes made to your trust—for example, if you need to change a beneficiary or back-up trustee—another attorney can do that for you. (Just make sure you again select an attorney with experience in living trusts.)

How Long Does It Take To Get A Living Trust Set Up?

Once you make the basic decisions—who will be your trustee, back-up trustees, beneficiaries, etc.— it should only take a couple of weeks for the attorney to prepare the first draft of the legal documents. Then you should plan on a couple more weeks to review them and have any changes made. Exactly how long it will take will depend on how quickly you respond, how much customizing needs to be done for your trust, and how busy your attorney is. Then, of course, you will need to change titles and beneficiary designations.

When Is A Good Time To Set Up A Living Trust?

Right now, while you are healthy and don't think you need one. Too many people put estate planning at the bottom of their priority list, when it really should be at the top. If you could make an appointment with disability or death, then you could put this off until then. But we all know that's not how it works.

If I Get A Living Trust, Have I Finished My Estate Planning?

Not necessarily. Depending on the size of your estate and your situation, you may need additional planning. If you have selected a qualified estate planning attorney to do your living trust, he/she will advise you as to whether or not you need additional planning and recommend some options for you to consider. We have included some of these options in Part Five so you can become familiar with them on your own time.

Do I Lose Control Of My Property If I Put It In A Living Trust?

Absolutely not. You keep full control over your property. You can do everything you could do before—buy and sell property, make changes, even cancel your trust at any time. Even if you name someone else as trustee, you can replace them at any time if you're not happy with the way your trust is being managed.

Will Putting Real Property Into My Living Trust Trigger A Re-Assessment Of The Property?

Land, and property that is "permanently attached" to land (such as a building or house), is called real property. In most states, retitling real property into the name of your trust will not cause it to be re-assessed or disturb the current mortgage in any way. As we explained on page 60, that's because you are not selling the property—you are merely correcting or amending the title.

Who Transfers The Property Into My Living Trust?

Most attorneys will automatically transfer the title of your home to your living trust for you. Usually, for an additional fee, the attorney will change other titles for you. If your attorney doesn't provide this service, he/she should, at least, provide you with instructions and assistance when needed. In any event, you are responsible for making sure all titles and appropriate beneficiary designations are changed to your living trust.

What Wording Should I Use For Property Titles And Beneficiary Designations?

Your attorney will tell you the exact wording you should use, but it will probably be something like this:

If you are single:

> "(your name), Trustee under trust dated (insert date you signed your trust)."

If you are married:

> "(your name) and (your spouse's name), Trustees under trust dated (insert date you signed your trust)."

Very often you will see the letters "UTD" used as a shortened version of the words "under trust dated." You may also see the letters "UA" which stand for "under agreement."

What Do I Do With My IRA?

Your trust can't be the owner of your IRA (that would disturb its tax-deferred status), but it can be the beneficiary. However, as we explain on page 61, if you are married there may be valid tax reasons for you to name your spouse as first beneficiary and your living trust as second beneficiary. This would also apply to other tax-deferred savings you may have, such as a 401(k) plan and other savings/retirement plans provided by your employer.

When I Put My Home In My Living Trust, Do I Lose The One-Time $125,000 Capital Gains Exemption?

No. It doesn't matter whether you or your trust owns your home—you still qualify for the one-time capital gains exemption when you sell your home.

When I Transfer My Bank And Savings Accounts To My Living Trust, Are They Still Insured?

Yes. Any account you have at an institution which is insured by the FDIC will continue to be insured when you change the title to your living trust—up to $100,000 per account.

If I Use A Corporate Trustee, Do I Lose Control Of My Property?

Not at all. Remember, you are still the grantor (the person setting up the trust), so you can make any changes you want to your trust at any time. If, for any reason, you are unhappy with the corporate trustee you have selected, you can replace them at any time.

If you are thinking about using a corporate trustee, you will want to evaluate their services and investment performance before naming one as trustee or co-trustee. Keep in mind that selecting a corporate trustee to act with you now is a good way for you to see how they will perform when you are no longer able to manage your trust yourself. See page 106 for more information.

When Will I Need To Update My Living Trust?

You should change your trust any time it no longer is what you want. Any major change in your family—such as marriage, divorce (especially if *you* marry or divorce), death, adoption, birth, etc.—should cause you to think about your trust. If one of your back-up trustees or guardians for your minor children can no longer fulfill their responsibilities (if they move away, become ill or die, or change their mind), you should replace them. It's a good idea to review your living trust at least every year (such as at the beginning of the year).

When you do need to change something in your trust document, don't write on the original document. Once you have signed the trust document and it has been notarized, it must not be altered. Your attorney will need to prepare an amendment to your trust that will be signed by you and notarized.

Remember that if you keep a separate list of your Special Gifts (specific items you want to go to certain people or organizations), you do not need to make any changes to your living trust document. You just need to update the list and have it notarized.

Do I Have To Have My Attorney Amend My Trust If I Buy Or Sell Property?

No. If you sell any property that's titled in your trust's name, you just need to sign the deed as the trustee of your trust. If you buy any new property, you just need to title the property in the name of your trust.

What If I Buy Property In Another State?

Before you buy property in another state (especially real estate), check to make sure it can be titled the same way as your trust property in your home state. A bank or title insurance company in the state where the property is located can usually tell you if the title you want to use is acceptable in that state.

What If I Move To Another State?

Most states follow the same general rules. But it's important to take your documents to a local attorney (use the process on page 124 to find a new attorney) and have him/her review them just to make sure no changes need to be made for that state. If something does need to be changed, make sure that only those parts are changed that need to be under the laws of that state. You don't need to pay another attorney to do a completely new document—unless, perhaps, if you move to Louisiana.

What's Different About Louisiana?

America's legal system, for the most part, is based on English common law (which makes sense, considering our history). However, Louisiana was part of the French territory, and its laws are still based on French or civil law. (For you history buffs, it's also called *Napoleonic code*—after Napoleon's attempt to standardize the legal system for his empire.)

For this reason, there are some major differences in the way the probate system works there. A living trust *is* valid in Louisiana, but if you live there you should definitely have an experienced estate planning attorney involved with your trust—even more so if you move to Louisiana from another state.

Where Should I Keep My Living Trust Documents?

You'll probably receive two originals of your living trust. You should keep one original trust document in your safe deposit box or another safe place. (Make sure your safe deposit box is titled in the name of your trust so your back-up trustee will have no trouble gaining access.) You may want to keep the other trust original with this book at home so you can review it from time to time. You don't want to keep both original trust documents in the same place, because they could be misplaced, lost in a fire, etc.

Do I Need To Give A Copy Of My Trust To Anyone?

No. If you want to, you can give a copy to each of your back-up trustees so they will be familiar with the document. (Make sure you tell them where the original documents are located.) But you do not need to give a copy to anyone or file it anywhere for it to be effective. (All you need to do to make your trust effective is sign the document, have it notarized, and change titles and appropriate beneficiary designations to your trust.)

As we mentioned in Part Four, your banker or investment broker may ask to see a copy of your trust when you change titles on your accounts—although you are under no legal obligation to do so. If it bothers you for them to see the full document, you can try showing them the Certificate of Trust your attorney prepares (see page 122 for more information). In many cases, this will satisfy their requirement, but some may still insist on seeing the complete document.

What About Adding Another Person On My Accounts Or Deeds After I Set Up My Trust?

Never add another person (including your parents or children) on the titles of your property or accounts—unless, of course, this person is your co-trustee—without first checking with your attorney. It could cause you or your family some very serious problems—possibly even defeating the purpose of your trust, or exposing you to a lawsuit.

Do I Put Instructions For My Funeral/Burial, Organ Donations, Etc. In My Living Trust?

These kinds of things you don't need to put in your living trust. It's a good idea, instead, to write them down in a separate letter (make sure you date it) or a separate document (a durable power of attorney for health care usually includes instructions for medical decisions like donation of organs). Then make copies and give one to each of your family members and back-up trustees to make sure they know your wishes. You can make changes to these instructions at any time without having to change your living trust document.

Who Decides If I Am Physically or Mentally Incapacitated Enough For My Back-up Trustee To Take Over?

Actually, you do—when you set up your living trust. Your trust will specify how many and what kinds of doctors need to examine you and verify your capacity to manage your business affairs. This can be as stringent or lenient

as you want to make it—for example, you may require only a statement from your family doctor; additional concurring statement(s) from one or more specialists; or an objective second or third opinion from an M.D. You can also list the doctors by name (this prevents any kind of "conspiracy" by relatives to have you declared incompetent by doctors who don't know you).

Does A Living Trust Reduce Income Taxes?

No. Income taxes must be paid on any income you receive each year, including the year in which you die. A living trust does not have any effect on the amount of income taxes you must pay. You may be confusing income taxes with federal *estate* taxes (also called death taxes because they are paid after you die). Estate taxes are different from, and in addition to, income taxes. With proper planning, your living trust *can* reduce or even eliminate estate taxes. You may want to refer to Part Three for a full explanation.

We Have An A-B Trust In Our Will. Doesn't This Do The Same Thing As An A-B Living Trust?

An A-B trust in a will does reduce or eliminate estate taxes in the same way as an A-B living trust. But, because the trust is part of a will, *it does not avoid probate*—the will must go through the entire probate procedure before the trust can even go into effect. On the other hand, an A-B living trust reduces or eliminates estate taxes—*and it also avoids probate.*

Why Do I Need To Set Up A Living Trust Now? Can't My Spouse Do This After I Die?

Your spouse can certainly set up his/her own living trust after you're gone, but that won't prevent your spouse from having to go through probate when you die. It would also be too late then to set up valuable tax planning that can save your family thousands of dollars. In addition, you could end up losing control over who receives your share of the estate (if this is a concern of yours, see page 86 for more information). And there's always the chance you will become incapacitated for some time before you die—do you want your spouse to have to deal with a conservatorship? These are only a few good reasons to plan now—while you are both alive and able.

My Spouse Is In A Nursing Home. Can I Set Up An A-B Living Trust For Us Now?

If your spouse is still capable of handling his/her own business affairs, you can certainly set up a common A-B living trust now. If your spouse is incompetent, you may still have some estate planning options. At the very least, you can and should set up a living trust for your share of the estate. See page 87 for more information.

I've Heard That Our Entire Estate Must Be Consumed In Order To Qualify For Government Benefits If My Spouse Or I Become Seriously Ill Or Injured. Does A Living Trust Provide Any Protection For This?

An A-B living trust can provide some protection, but only after one spouse has died. It can be set up so that only Trust A (the surviving spouse's trust) will need to be consumed in order to qualify for these benefits, allowing the assets in Trust B (the deceased's trust) to be preserved for the beneficiaries. See page 87 for more information.

My Spouse Isn't A U.S. Citizen. Can We Still Have A Living Trust?

Yes, but there have been some recent changes in the tax laws and your spouse is no longer entitled to the marital deduction. This means that, without proper planning, anything over $600,000 in your estate will be taxed. As part of an A-B provision in your living trust, you need something called a "qualified domestic trust" with your living trust. Make sure your attorney knows that your spouse is not a U.S. citizen before your trust is prepared.

I'm Not Married. Can I Have An A-B Living Trust To Save On Estate Taxes?

No, only a married couple can benefit from the tax planning in an A-B living trust. That's because an A-B living trust uses the marital deduction as part of its tax-planning—and the marital deduction is only available if you are married. If you need tax planning, you may be interested in some of the options discussed in Part Five. Your attorney will be able to give you some recommendations for your situation.

Does A Living Trust Protect My Assets From Creditors?

No, a living trust does not shield your assets from creditors.

I'm A Doctor And, Since I Could Be Sued For Malpractice, I've Heard I Should Have A Will Instead Of A Living Trust. Is This True?

No, you can and should have a living trust. You probably heard this because probate limits the time a creditor has to present a claim against an estate. In some states now, a living trust can also provide this. But if this isn't the case where you live, the trustee of your trust can simply open a probate when you die to see if any creditors have claims to present. If they do, then he/she would transfer out of your living trust *just enough assets to satisfy the claim(s)*—the rest would stay in your living trust, protected from probate. See page 69 for a full discussion.

My Accountant Says I Have To Use A Separate Tax Identification Number And File A Separate Income Tax Return For My Living Trust. Is This True?

Not for a *revocable* living trust, which is what this book is primarily about.

A living trust is a trust that is created while you are living. And there are two kinds of living trusts—a *revocable* living trust (which can be changed or cancelled at any time) and an *irrevocable* living trust (which cannot be changed once the document has been signed, such as a life insurance trust or a charitable remainder trust, both of which are explained in Part Five).

Because the IRS considers an irrevocable trust to be a separate entity from the grantor (the person who sets up the trust), it *does* require a separate tax identification number and separate tax return for these. However, because a revocable living trust can be changed or cancelled by the grantor at any time, it does not have to meet the same requirements as an irrevocable trust.

If you are married, as long as you and/or your spouse are the grantors of your revocable living trust, at least one of you is a trustee or co-trustee, *and* you file a joint income tax return, you do not need to file a separate tax return or have a separate tax identification number. You simply continue to use your social security number as the tax identification number (just as you have in the past) and you continue to file your regular joint income tax return. If you have an A-B (or A-B-C) living trust, when one spouse dies Trust B (and Trust C)

become irrevocable—so then a separate tax identification number and tax return are required.

Along these same lines, if you are the sole grantor of your revocable living trust, as long as you are the trustee or co-trustee, you continue to use your social security number and file your regular tax return.

If your accountant has a question about this, he/she may want to review Section 1.671-4 and Section 301.6109-1 of the Income Tax Regulations.

A Living Trust Almost Sounds Too Good To Be True. Isn't There Anything Bad About It?

No, there really isn't. As we mentioned in Part Two, you *may* experience some inconveniences, but these are very minor—especially when compared to the many advantages a living trust provides.

Usually the only problem people have with properly prepared living trusts is with property that was left out of them—because they failed to change titles and beneficiary designations. The trusts still work—but any property left out of them usually ends up having to be probated.

It does take a little extra effort and some time on your part to change titles and beneficiary designations, but once it's done it's easy to maintain—and your family will be very appreciative.

How Do I Know Congress Won't Eliminate Living Trusts?

Anything's possible, but it's highly unlikely. Remember, living trusts have been around, in one form or another, for hundreds of years. Besides, neither the state nor federal government receives income from probate, so there's no incentive for them to eliminate living trusts and make people go through probate. In fact, the states have every reason to *encourage* living trusts as a way to reduce the already overcrowded court system.

However, estate taxes *are* a source of revenue for the federal government, so it's more likely that Congress will change the amount of the federal estate tax exemption, which it has done in the past. In fact, there currently is some talk of lowering the exemption from $600,000 to $300,000. That would make living trusts even more popular, as more people with smaller estates would

now have to worry about estate taxes and could benefit from the tax planning in an A-B living trust.

A Closing Note About The Common A-B Living Trust

As we mentioned earlier in Part Three, there are some attorneys who don't think you can have one common A-B living trust and use both $600,000 estate tax exemptions. However, many experienced estate planning attorneys write common A-B living trust documents all the time, using both exemptions just as we've explained.

Of course, as we've also mentioned, there may be valid reasons for your attorney to recommend that you and your spouse have separate living trusts. But if your attorney tells you this *can't* be done, you may want to get a second opinion. You may also want to keep reading to understand more about this difference in opinions.

Your attorney may be referring to section 2036(a) of the Internal Revenue Code. (This gets a little technical, so bear with us.) This section of the tax code basically says that if you retain certain rights during your lifetime to property that you transfer into a trust (including the right to receive income from the trust), that property will be included in your taxable estate when you die.

Your attorney may take the position that because the surviving spouse moves (transfers) the assets from the common trust to Trust A and Trust B after the first spouse dies, then *the surviving spouse* is the one making the transfer. And since he/she can also receive income from Trust B, then it appears that Trust B must be included in the surviving spouse's taxable estate at his/her death and would not be entitled to the first spouse's estate tax exemption.

The key issue here is *who* is making the transfer. In the common A-B living trust that we talk about, the surviving spouse is *not* the one making the transfer. The trust document includes a provision that when the first spouse dies, the common trust *automatically* splits into two separate trusts. And since it is the death of this spouse that causes the common trust to split, *the first spouse to die* is the one making the transfer—not the surviving spouse. The surviving spouse as trustee is simply following the instructions in the trust document when he/she divides the assets between Trust A and Trust B.

Since the first spouse to die is the one making the transfer, Trust B *remains* the property of that spouse and is entitled to a $600,000 exemption. Trust A, of course, uses the surviving spouse's exemption later when he/she dies.

Another key issue is how the trust document says you own the trust property when the first spouse dies. For example, if the trust document uses wording that is similar to *joint tenancy with right of survivorship*, when the first spouse dies, the surviving spouse will automatically own everything in the trust. So any property that is placed into Trust B is no longer the property of the deceased—it is now the property of the surviving spouse. So there is nothing that the deceased's estate tax exemption can be applied toward.

But if the wording is similar to *tenancy in common*, then the property stays separate and will not transfer to the surviving spouse. This allows each grantor to retain ownership of his/her share of the trust property, so each exemption can be used. (You may want to refer back to page 19 where we discuss these two kinds of ownership.)

If you live in a community property state, this is done by retaining the community property status of the equal shares of the property.

You can see how important it is that your trust document is prepared by someone with experience. If you want to get a second opinion, you may want to refer back to Part Four for some guidelines on how to find an experienced estate planning attorney to do your living trust.

Part Seven

GETTING ORGANIZED

Part Seven— GETTING ORGANIZED

INSTRUCTIONS FOR COMPLETING THE PERSONAL AND FINANCIAL ORGANIZER

To set up your living trust, your attorney will need some basic information about you. The Personal and Financial Organizer has been designed to help you prepare for your meeting with your attorney by providing one place for you to put all the information your attorney will need to prepare your living trust document. Being organized will undoubtedly save you time and money.

Completing the Organizer and actually writing this information down will also help you to think seriously about your plan. These are very important decisions you are making—who will be your trustee, back-up trustee(s), beneficiaries, how you want your children to inherit, what you want to happen if you become incompetent, etc.—so you will want to take your time and give careful consideration to your options. You may want to re-read sections of the book that apply to each decision (we've included page numbers whenever appropriate, making it easy for you to find those sections). If you are married, you and your spouse should discuss your options openly and try to make your decisions *together*.

In addition, you should take the time to complete the Organizer as much as possible *before* you meet with your attorney. However, you will probably have some questions you will want to ask your attorney, and you may want to discuss some of your options with him/her before actually making a

decision. So be sure to make notes in the appropriate section or write your questions down in Section 8 so you won't forget about them. At the same time, keep in mind that this is *your* plan. Your attorney will only be able to give you options and make suggestions for you to consider—only *you* (and your spouse) can make the actual decisions about *your* living trust.

Here are a few general instructions. Print or write *legibly*. Using a pencil is a good idea, since you will probably make some changes. If you don't have enough room on the Organizer to put all the information requested, use a separate sheet of paper and attach it to that page. If a question doesn't apply to you, mark "N/A" for "not applicable" rather than leaving it blank—this way your attorney will know that you did not overlook the question or forget to answer it. And, here's a final reminder. *Take your time* completing this Organizer—these are *serious* personal decisions.

Now, let's complete the Organizer.

SECTION 1 GENERAL INFORMATION

Be sure to date the organizer and mark your marital status. If you are single, you only need to complete the sections that apply to you. If you are married, you and your spouse need to complete this entire section.

SECTION 2 PERSONAL INFORMATION

This section requests some basic information that will help introduce your family situation to your attorney—if you have children, stepchildren, brothers/sisters and if you have any dependents who require special care. It will also let your attorney know if you expect to receive property or money from an outside source (which would increase the value of your estate).

In general, this information gives your attorney insight into situations that could develop later on, and it will be invaluable in planning your living trust.

For example, if your spouse is not a U.S. citizen, your attorney may need to include an additional provision in your trust document.

If you have a previous will or trust that this living trust will replace, make sure you take a copy with you when you meet with your attorney. And if you have special circumstances that are not included here and you feel your attorney needs to know about them, make a note in this section or in Section 8—or attach a separate sheet of paper.

SECTION 3 FINANCIAL INFORMATION

This section will give your attorney an accurate current net value of your estate (the market value of everything you own less what you owe), so he/she will be able to know if you need tax planning in your living trust. It will also give your attorney insight into the kinds of titles and beneficiary designations that will need to be changed. If the attorney doesn't change these for you, at least he/she will be able to give you all the information you will need to change them easily and correctly. It will be a good check list for you, too, to help you make sure you change *all* of them.

We've included space for you to write down in whose name each asset is titled. Depending on how much property you and your spouse own separately, your attorney may recommend that you have separate living trusts in addition to or instead of a common living trust.

You'll notice on Questions 1 and 5 that we have included a place for you to list the purchase price (cost basis) of these assets. This will let your attorney know if you have a potential capital gains problem. If so, he/she may recommend some additional tax planning options for you to consider (some of these are in Part Five). Remember, a *gain* is the same thing as profit—the difference between what you get when you sell an asset and what you paid for it when you bought it. When you sell an asset, the gain is included as income in that year—and you have to pay income taxes on it.

You'll also notice on Questions 1 and 2 that we've included a "ready made" formula to help you determine the equity in these assets. Remember, we're interested in the *net* value of your estate. So you will list the current market value of each asset, and subtract from that the remaining mortgage or loan value, which gives you the equity (or net value) of that asset. You may need to have some current appraisals done if an asset has not been appraised recently (especially real estate).

It is very important that you fully complete this section. Make sure you include any separately owned property and that you list the appropriate owner. If you need more room to answer any of the questions in Section 3, list them on a separate sheet of paper and attach it to these pages.

4 TRUST DECISIONS: YOUR LIVING TRUST TEAM

Okay, so far this has been pretty easy. Beginning in this section, you will need to give some very serious thought to your living trust plan.

1. Trustee(s)

See page 101 for more information.
Your trustee is responsible for management of your trust now. You can be your own trustee if you want to. If you are married, you and your spouse can be co-trustees. You can also name someone else as your trustee or co-trustee—an adult son or daughter, other relative, or a corporate trustee. You should probably consider naming someone else as your trustee or co-trustee if you don't have the time, ability, or desire to manage your own affairs anymore or if you and/or your spouse are ill. (Remember, until you become incompetent or die, you can always change your trustee.)

2. Back-Up Trustee(s)

See page 102 for more information.
Your back-up trustee will step in and take control for you if you become physically or mentally incapacitated and are no longer able to handle your own affairs. When you die, your back-up acts just like an executor in a will does—pays your final bills and distributes your property according to the

instructions in your trust. If you have a co-trustee (perhaps your spouse), he/she will assume these responsibilities until his/her own incapacity or death, at which time your back-up trustee will take over.

You will probably want to name two or three back-up trustees if, for whatever reason, the first is not available. They should be people you know and trust, whose judgment you respect and who will also respect your wishes. They do not have to live in the same state you do, although it would be helpful if they live close to you. If you have adult children, they can be named as back-up trustees.

If you wish, you can name two or more back-up trustees to jointly share the responsibilities (for instance, you may want two of your adult children to act together). You may also want to consider naming a third impartial co-back-up trustee (like a corporate trustee) to prevent any deadlocks or major disagreements. If you do want to name two or more to act together, just cross out "1st choice," "2nd choice," and "3rd choice" and write in "Co-trustees" as appropriate.

If you don't feel you have good candidates as back-ups—your family lives too far away, they're too busy or aren't responsible enough, or if you feel you have no one you can trust—you should probably select a corporate trustee as your back-up trustee.

3. Guardians For Minor Children

See page 109 for more information.

If you have minor children, you will need to select a guardian for them. This is a very important decision. The person you name will be *responsible for raising* your children if both parents are dead or incompetent. Guardians must be adults. You will, of course, want to choose someone who respects your values and standards (moral, ethical and religious) and will raise your children the way you would want.

Remember, the court must still approve your selection. If you are a single parent with custody and really don't want your "ex" to be guardian, go ahead and name your preference anyway. While the other natural parent is almost always the court's preferred choice, your choice will receive careful consideration. It's possible that the other parent may not be able to take the

responsibility (or won't want it), or the court could agree with you that he/she is not a suitable choice. In these situations, the judge would want to know your preference.

4. Trustees For Minor Children

See page 109 for more information.

Remember, the guardian is only responsible for *raising* your children and does not control the inheritance. You also need to name a trustee for your children's trust—someone who will be responsible for the safekeeping of their inheritance, and will provide the money for education, medical care, maintenance and other needs from the assets in the children's trust.

Many parents name the same person as trustee and guardian, making it convenient for one person to take care of your children. However, a children's trustee *can* be a different individual, a corporate trustee or, if you wish, you can name two as co-trustees.

SECTION

5 BENEFICIARIES

Your beneficiaries are the persons and organizations who will receive your property and possessions when you die. Most people prefer to pass their property down to family members, but you can leave it to any person or organization you wish. If you are married and you want to make sure the beneficiaries you have named cannot be changed if you die first, ask your attorney about including an A-B provision in your common living trust (see Part Three for more information).

1. Special Gifts—Organizations

See page 119 for more information.

This is an excellent time to think about giving to a favorite charity or organization that has special meaning to you. There are many excellent ones and they are all in need of funding to continue their work. In addition to the tax benefits of charitable donations, you will have the satisfaction of knowing that your contribution will make a difference. Your gift can be as specific or as general, as large or as small, as you want to make it. The charity or foundation of your choice will be glad to make suggestions.

2. Special Gifts—Individuals

See page 118 for more information.

You probably will want to leave specific items to certain individuals—a favorite piece of jewelry or antique that you want a special friend or relative to have. Remember, you just need to make a list of these Special Gifts on a separate sheet of paper, have it notarized, and keep it with your living trust document. If you change your mind, just make a new list and have it notarized. You may want to make a separate list for each of your children or grandchildren.

Use the space on this Organizer to start getting your Special Gifts lists organized. This way, if you have any questions, you will be prepared when you meet with your attorney.

3. Beneficiaries

See page 108 for more information.

Who do you want to receive the rest of your property and possessions after your Special Gifts have been distributed? For most people, this will probably be the bulk of your estate—your home, other real estate, investments, etc.—everything that you did not list as a Special Gift. Remember, it's usually better to specify a percentage rather than a dollar amount.

4. Inheriting Instructions

See page 111 for more information.

When do you want your children to inherit? You may want to keep "strings" on their inheritance until each child reaches an age at which you feel he/she will be mature enough to have outright control, such as age 21 or 25. Some parents specify a certain amount at certain ages (some at 21, some at 25, etc.) or at certain intervals (some every three to five years). It's completely up to you. You just need to specify how long you want the trustee(s) to keep control.

5. Dependents Who Require Special Care

See page 113 for more information.

If you have a disabled child or other dependent who requires special care, your attorney will need to know how you want to provide for them and any other special instructions you may have.

6. Alternate Beneficiaries

See page 118 for more information.

Who would you want to have your property if all of the people you have named as your beneficiaries die before you? Many people specify their church, a favorite charity, or foundation.

7. Disinheriting

See page 118 for more information.

Are there any persons that you specifically want to exclude? Make sure you write them down.

SECTION

6 SPECIAL INSTRUCTIONS FOR INCOMPETENCY

This is a very appropriate time to think about what you would want to happen to you and your property if you were to become physically or mentally incapacitated and unable to handle your own affairs. You may have some specific requests and/or instructions if this should happen to you—and your co-trustee or back-up trustee(s), family members, and physicians should know your wishes.

1. Keeping/Selling Assets

If you become incompetent, it may be necessary to liquidate some of your assets to pay for your care. Do you have a preference for which ones are sold first? Are there others you don't want sold unless absolutely necessary? Do you have any special instructions you want followed? Are there any potential buyers you would want contacted? In addition, you may want some special gifts distributed at this time.

2. Medical Care

You may have specific requests regarding your medical care. For example, you may want to be cared for in a specific hospital or nursing home (or maybe there's one you don't want to be in). You may also have some definite ideas about the type or extent of care you receive at this time—life support, blood transfusions, organ transplants, etc.

3. Living Will/Durable Power of Attorney For Health Care

See page 123 for more information.

This is a good time to think about what you would want to happen if you become terminally ill or injured with no hope for recovery. A durable power of attorney for health care is usually preferred, but it is not available in all states. A living will, which will at least make your wishes known, is recognized in just about all states. Be sure to ask your attorney if these are available in your state.

SECTION 7 SPECIAL INSTRUCTIONS FOR FUNERAL/BURIAL

Although this information will not be included in your actual trust document, we have included this section on the Organizer to help you think about these things now. It will be much easier for you to make these decisions now than to expect your family to make them at a very emotional (and vulnerable) time. You will want to put this information, along with your instructions for a service, etc., in a letter or on a separate piece of paper, date it and sign it. Make copies and give them to your family members, co-trustee and back-up trustees.

SECTION 8 QUESTIONS TO ASK YOUR ATTORNEY ABOUT YOUR LIVING TRUST

This is where you can list the questions you have about your living trust, so you won't forget to ask your attorney.

SUMMARY

There—now you've got your information all organized. That was a big step. Now it's time to see an estate planning attorney who can answer your questions and prepare your living trust documents for you. (Remember to take this book and your completed Personal and Financial Organizer with you.) We suggest that you re-read pages 124-129 if you don't yet have an attorney selected. Good luck—and good for you for taking care of this now!

IN CONCLUSION

We hope we've told you enough about probate that you'll want to make sure you and your family are protected from it. You should also understand living trusts enough now that you'll feel comfortable getting one for yourself. You may even find yourself telling your neighbors, friends and relatives all about the problems with probate and the advantages of a living trust—and we think that would be wonderful!

We have spent a great amount of time trying to make this book simple enough for everyone to understand, yet complete enough to give you enough information that you can intelligently ask the questions you want to ask. And, we hope, the book is interesting enough that you have finished reading it!

Please share this book with the rest of your family and your friends—even better, send them a copy of their own. It could be one of the most important gifts you ever give to those you care about.

Don't postpone protecting your family. None of us can know when tragedy will strike, and once it does it's too late. A sudden tragic accident or illness can put you and/or your family under the control of the probate court for years. Now you know what that can mean—and you know how to prevent it.

Please act now.

PERSONAL AND FINANCIAL ORGANIZER FOR YOUR LIVING TRUST

SECTION 1 GENERAL INFORMATION

DATE: ______________________

Marital Status: Married Single Divorced Widowed

Your Name (First, Middle, Last)	Soc. Sec. No.	Date of Birth	
Spouse's Name (First, Middle, Last)	Soc. Sec. No.	Date of Birth	
Home Address (Number, Street)	City	State	Zip
Mailing Address If Different From Above (Number, Street)	City	State	Zip
( ) Home Phone	( ) Your Work Phone	( ) Spouse's Work Phone	
Your Employer	Your Occupation		
Employer's Address (Number, Street)	City	State	Zip
Spouse's Employer	Spouse's Occupation		
Spouse's Employer's Address (Number, Street)	City	State	Zip

SECTION 2 PERSONAL INFORMATION

	You		Your Spouse	
1. Are you a U.S. citizen?	Yes	No	Yes	No
2. Do you have a will or trust now?	Yes	No	Yes	No
3. Are you expecting to receive property or money from (circle all that apply):	Gift Lawsuit	Inheritance Other	Gift Lawsuit	Inheritance Other
If so, approximately how much?	$ ________		$ ________	
4. How many living children do you have?				
5. How many deceased children do you have?				
6. Are all your children legally yours (natural or legally adopted)?	Yes	No	Yes	No
7. How many stepchildren do you have?				
8. How many children under age 18 do you have?				
9. How many children under age 25 do you have?				
10. Do you have any dependents who require special care?	Yes	No	Yes	No
If so, how are they related to you and how old are they?				
11. How many grandchildren do you have?				
12. How many of your brothers and sisters are still living?				

SECTION

3 FINANCIAL INFORMATION

1. Do you own a **home** or any **other real estate**?

Description and Location	Titled in whose name	Purchase Price	Market Value	(-) Mortgage	(=) Equity
				Total Net Value	

2. Do you own any **other titled property** such as a car, boat, etc.?

Description	Titled in whose name	Market Value	(-) Mortgage	(=) Equity
			Total Net Value	

3. Do you have any **checking accounts**?

Name of Bank	Titled in whose name	Approx. Balance
	Total Value	

4. Do you have any **interest bearing accounts** (savings, money market) and/or **CDs**?

Name of Bank	Titled in whose name	Approx. Balance
	Total Value	

5. Do you own any **stocks, bonds or mutual funds** (including company stock)?

# of Shares	Name of Security	Titled in whose name	Purchase Price	Current Value
			Total Value	

6. Do you have any **profit sharing, IRAs or pension plans**?

Description/Location	Beneficiary	Current Value
	Total Value	

7. Do you have any **life insurance** policies and/or **annuities**?

Name of Company	Policy Owner	1st Beneficiary	2nd Beneficiary	Death Benefit
			Total Value	

8. Does anyone owe you money?

Description	Approx. Value
Total Value	

9. Do you have any **special items of value** such as coin collections, antiques, jewelry, etc.?

Description	Approx. Value
Total Value	

10. What is the approximate total value of all your remaining **personal property**—whatever you own that has not been included above? (clothes, furniture, etc.) Just estimate. .... $ ________

11. Do you have any **debts** other than mortgage(s) and loans listed above (credit cards, personal loans, etc.)?

	Amount owed
Total Debt	

12. Total value of everything you (and your spouse) own (add totals of line 1 thru line 10 above) ....$ ________

13. Total amount you (and your spouse) owe (total of line 11 above) .... — ________

14. Subtract line 13 from line 12. **TOTAL NET ESTATE VALUE =** $ ________

15. Do you have a **safe deposit box**?

Location	Titled in whose name

SECTION

4 TRUST DECISIONS: YOUR LIVING TRUST TEAM

1. **Trustee(s)**—Manages your trust now; usually you (and your spouse) and/or a corporate trustee.

____

2. **Back-up Trustee(s)**—Steps in at your disability or death. Can be your adult children, trusted friends, and/or a corporate trustee.

#1 Choice: Name ____________________

Address ____________________

#2 Choice: Name ____________________

Address ____________________

#3 Choice: Name ____________________

Address ____________________

3. **Guardians For Minor Children**—Responsible adult who will raise your children if something happens to you.

#1 Choice: Name ____________________

Address ____________________

#2 Choice: Name ____________________

Address ____________________

4. **Trustees For Minor Children**— Manages your children's inheritance. Can be the same person as the guardian, another adult and/or a corporate trustee.

#1 Choice: Name ____________________

Address ____________________

#2 Choice: Name ____________________

Address ____________________

SECTION

5 BENEFICIARIES

1. **Special Gifts To Organizations**

Do you want to make a gift (cash or a specific item) to a charity, foundation, religious or fraternal organization?

Name of Organization	Description of Gift

2. **Special Gifts To Individuals**

Do you want to give any specific items to a family member or other individual? (For example: wedding ring to your daughter, gun collection to a son or nephew, etc.)

Name of Person	Description of Gift

3. **Beneficiaries**

Who do you want to receive the rest of your estate after these special gifts have been distributed? You can designate a dollar amount or a percentage.

Name of Person/Organization	Amount/Percentage

4. **Inheriting Instructions**

Do you want your children to receive their inheritance in installments, at certain ages, or all at once?

5. **Dependents Who Require Special Care**

Do you want to provide for "basic" care or luxuries and other extras to supplement government benefits?

6. **Alternate Beneficiaries**

Who do you want to receive your estate if you (and your spouse) outlive the beneficiaries you've named above?

Name of Person/Organization	Amount/Percentage

7. **Disinheriting**

Are there any relatives that you specifically do not want to receive anything from your estate?

SECTION 6 SPECIAL INSTRUCTIONS FOR INCOMPETENCY

1. **Keeping/Selling Assets**
   If necessary to pay for your care, do you want certain assets sold first? Are there potential buyers you want contacted?

2. **Medical Care**
   Do you want to be in (or avoid) a certain hospital/nursing home? How do you feel about blood transfusions, organ transplants, life support, etc?

You ______________________________

Your Spouse ______________________________

3. A **Living Will** makes your wishes known to family and doctors regarding life support in the event you become terminally ill or injured with no hope for recovery. Do you want a living will?

You		Your Spouse	
Yes	No	Yes	No

A **Durable Power of Attorney For Health Care,** if available in your state, gives broader protection. Ask your attorney.

SECTION 7 SPECIAL INSTRUCTIONS FOR FUNERAL/BURIAL

1. What type of service do you want, how elaborate, and where? Any special people to contact? Do you want cremation?

2. If you have a cemetery lot, where is it located? ______________________________
   Cemetery Name City State

SECTION 8 QUESTIONS TO ASK YOUR ATTORNEY ABOUT YOUR LIVING TRUST

DEFINITIONS

We've introduced a lot of terms that may be new to you, so we've put together this list as a handy reference. There are also some legal terms that we have purposely not used in this book because we wanted to keep it easy to understand. But since you will probably feel more comfortable dealing with an attorney if you know some of their "legalese," we've included some of it here.

Administrator—Person named by the court to represent the estate when there is no will or the will did not name an executor (female is administratix); also called a personal representative

Back-up Trustee—Also called successor trustee; person or institution named in the trust agreement who can take over should the first trustee die, resign or become unable to act

Beneficiaries—In a living trust, the persons and/or organizations who receive the trust property after the death of the trust grantor

Codicil—A written change or amendment to a will

Conservator/Guardian—One who is legally responsible for the care and well-being of another person; if appointed by a court, the conservator/guardian is under the court's supervision

Conservatorship—A court controlled program for persons who are unable to manage their own affairs (due to physical or mental incapacity). Also called a probate guardianship in some states.

Corporate Trustee—An institution (such as a bank or trust company) which specializes in the management of trusts

Cost Basis—What you paid for the property. The value that is used to determine gain or loss for income tax purposes. Property is given a *stepped-up basis* when transferred by inheritance (through a will or trust) and is re-valued as of the date of the owner's death

Crummey Letter—A written notification to the beneficiaries of an irrevocable life insurance trust that a gift has been received on their behalf; when the beneficiaries decline the gift, the funds can then be used to purchase insurance on the grantor's life

Durable Power Of Attorney—See Power of Attorney

Durable Power Of Attorney For Health Care—A document that gives someone else the legal authority to make health care decisions for you in the event you are unable to make them for yourself

Estate—Assets and debts left by an individual at death

Estate Taxes—Federal or state taxes on the value of the property left at death; often called inheritance tax or death tax

Executor—Person or institution named in a will to carry out its instructions (female is executrix); also called a personal representative

Fiduciary—Person having the legal duty to act primarily for another's benefit; implies great confidence and trust, and a high degree of good faith; (usually associated with a trustee)

Gain—The difference between what you receive for property when it is sold and what you paid for it; used to determine the amount of taxes due

Generation Skipping Transfer (GST) Tax—A steep tax (55%) levied on the assets that skip a generation and are left directly to grandchildren and younger generations; (everyone has a $1 million exemption from this tax)

Grantor—The person who sets up or creates the trust; also called the creator, settlor, or trustor

Gross Estate—The value of an estate before the debts are paid; (probate fees are usually calculated on the gross value of the estate)

Holographic Will—A handwritten will

Incapacitated/Incompetent—One who is unable to manage his/her own affairs, either temporarily or permanently; lack of legal power

Irrevocable Trust—Opposite of revocable trust; a trust that cannot be changed (revoked) or cancelled once it is set up

Intestate—Without a will

Joint Ownership—Also called joint tenancy; when two or more persons own the same property; death of a joint owner immediately transfers ownership to the surviving joint owners; different from tenancy-in-common (see below)

Living Will—A written document stating that you do not wish to be kept alive by artificial means when the illness or injury is terminal

Living Trust—A written legal document into which you place all of your property, with instructions for its management and distribution upon your disability or death; also known as a revocable inter vivos trust; a trust created during one's lifetime

Minor Child—A child under the legal age for an adult; varies by state (usually under 18 or 21)

Net Value—The value of an estate after all debts have been paid; (federal estate taxes are based on the net value of an estate)

Per Capita—A way of distributing your estate so that your surviving descendents will share equally, regardless of generation

Per Stirpes—A way of distributing your estate so that your surviving descendents will receive only what their immediate ancestor would have received if he/she had been alive at your death

Personal Property—Movable property (as opposed to real property which is permanent, such as land); includes furniture, automobiles, equipment, cash and stocks

Personal Representative—Another name for an executor or administrator

Power of Attorney—A legal document giving another person full legal authority to sign your name on your behalf in your absence (different from the fiduciary duty of a trustee); ends at disability or death; some states permit a durable power of attorney which is valid through disability and ends at death. These are general powers of attorney. There are also limited powers of attorney which give someone only limited authority for a very specific purpose (for example, to sell a car).

Probate—
With a will (see testate)—The legal process of filing a will with the probate court; the court determines if the will is valid, hears all claims, orders creditors paid and property distributed according to the terms of the will

Without a will (see intestate)—The legal process of the probate court receiving all claims, ordering creditors paid and property distributed according to the laws of that state (the state's will)

Probate Guardianship—A court controlled program to manage the affairs of minor children. (In some states, a conservatorship is also called a probate guardianship.)

Real Property—Land, and property which is "permanently" attached to land (such as a building or house)

Revocable Trust—Opposite of irrevocable trust; a trust in which the person setting it up retains the power to change (revoke) or cancel the trust during his/her lifetime

Simple Pour Over Will—A short will often used with a living trust; states that any property left out of your living trust will become part of ("pour over" into) your living trust upon your death

Special Gifts—A separate listing of special property

Spouse—Husband or wife

Tenancy-In-Common—A form of joint ownership in which two or more persons own the same property; at death of a tenant-in-common, ownership transfers to that person's heirs, not to the other owner; different from joint ownership/joint tenancy (see above)

Testamentary Trust—A trust set up in a will that only takes effect after death

Testate—One who dies with a will

Trustee—Person or institution agreeing to accept and manage property according to the instructions in the trust agreement

Will—A written document with instructions for disposing of property at death; can only be enforced through the probate court

INDEX

E

F

G

I

J

K

L

Marketing & Educational Materials

For Estate Planning Professionals

These marketing and educational materials, by the authors of *Understanding Living Trusts*, have been developed to help you explain the basic concepts of living, insurance & charitable remainder trusts to your staff and clients.

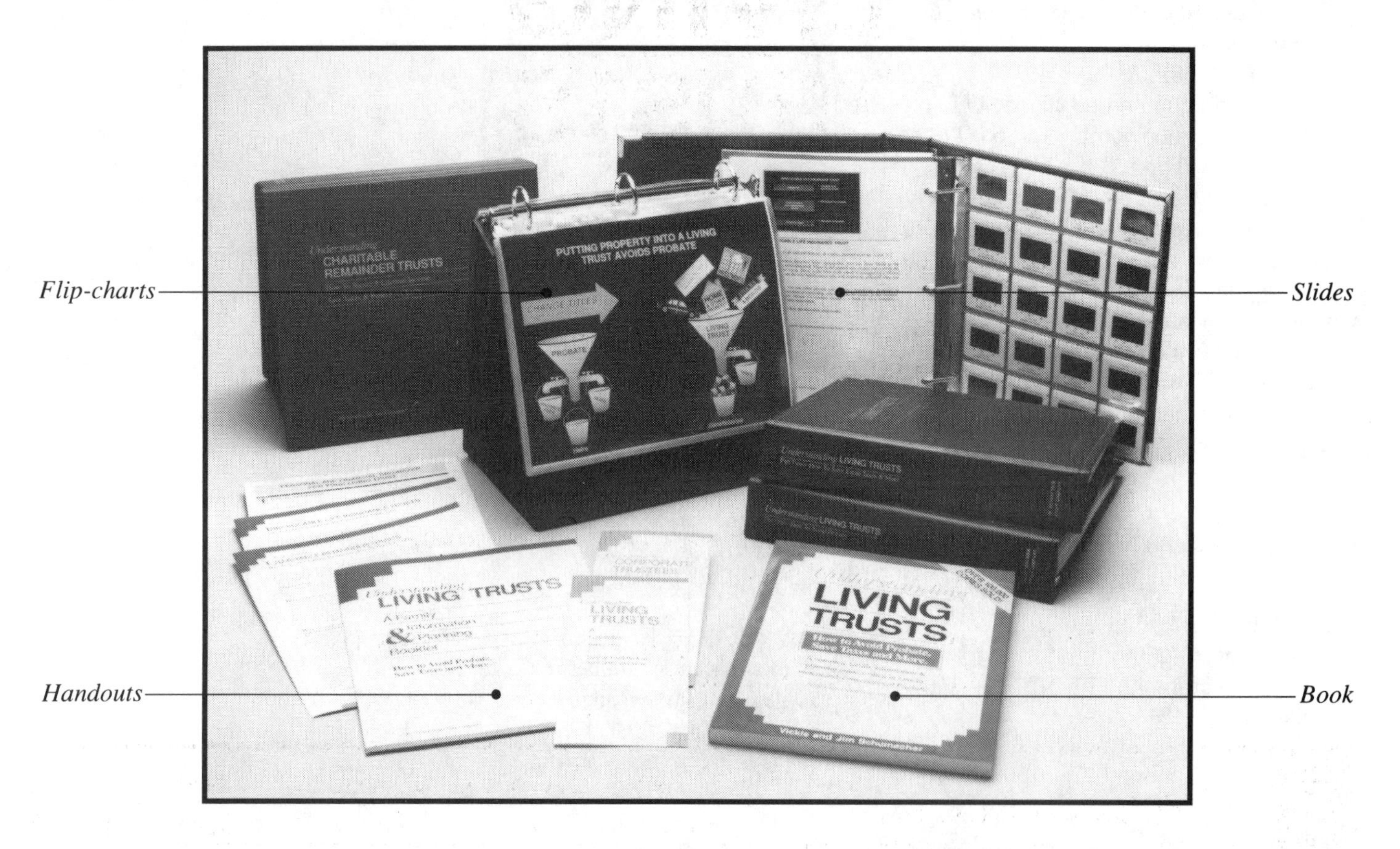

Here are some of the key benefits of using these powerful materials:

- ✓ Save valuable time—inform and motivate whole groups of prospects at once;
- ✓ Gain the competitive edge and enhance your professional image;
- ✓ Substantially increase your bottom line—attract more leads and more clients;
- ✓ Receive invitations to make professional presentations everywhere;
- ✓ Printed handout materials can be used separately or with slide and flip chart presentations for a complete professional package.

The definitive audio/visual marketing and educational aids for:

- ✓ Attorneys
- ✓ Banks & Trust Companies
- ✓ Charities
- ✓ Insurance Professionals
- ✓ Financial Advisors

- **Quality**
- **Accuracy**
- **Satisfaction**

100% Guaranteed

For more information, call or write:

SCHUMACHER AND COMPANY

1800 Century Park East • Suite 1250 • Los Angeles, CA 90067

(800) 728-2665 • FAX (310) 284-8951

(7:30 am - 5:30 pm Pacific Time)